INTRODUCTION TO SOCIAL WORK

&

PSYCHOLOGY FOR SOCIAL WORKERS

(SYLLABUS AND STUDY MATERIALS)

PROJECT MSW

DEPARTMENT OF SOCIAL WORK

PSG COLLEGE OF ARTS AND SCIENCE, COIMBATORE

CONTENTS BELONGS TO ALL STUDENTS OF SOCIAL WORK DEPARTMENT

(2012 – 2014 BATCH)

COMPILED BY: T.M.SURESH

CONTENTS COMPILED BY: G.SANTHOSH, THIVYA VILASHINI AND ALL MSW STUDENTS OF
SOCIAL WORK DEPARTMENT, PSG COLLEGE OF ARTS AND SCIENCE

SYLLABUS

UNIT – I

Psychology, meaning and fields of psychology – scientific methods of Psychology – relevant of Psychology for social work practices.

UNIT – II

Life span – physical, social and psychological aspects of development from prenatal period to old age. Motivation and hierarchy of needs

UNIT – III

Learning – meaning – theory of learning – the classical conditioning – operant conditioning cognitive learning – methods of effective learning – nature of memory forgetting – thinking – perception – concept and types – perception and sensation – characteristics of perception laws and perception grouping – errors in perception.

UNIT – IV INTELLINGENCE

Concepts and measurements of intelligence – theory of intelligence – mental health. Introduction to concept of mental health and classification of mental illness and retardation – mental deficiency.

UNIT – V PERSONALITY

Meaning – determinants of personalities – defense mechanism – theory of personality – measurement of personality. Adjustment – concept of adjustment and maladjustments – stress – frustration and conflict sources of frustration conflicts – nature and types of conflicts.

REFERENCE BOOKS:

General psychology – S.K. MANGAL.
Development psychology – B. Elizabeth Hurlock.

UNIT – I

Psychology, meaning and fields of psychology – scientific methods of Psychology – relevant of Psychology for social work practices.

INTRODUCTION

Psychology is a scientific discipline. It branched off from philosophy and has ushered as an independent science on its own right. The definition of psychology had undergone several revisions in the past. It is currently defined as a discipline engaged in studying behavior and mental processes. The field of psychology is ever expanding and diversifying. Several sub fields of psychology have been developed. The strength of psychology as a science rests on its methods. A wide variety of methods have been eve loved by psychologists over the century. These methods help collecting data needed to build up a reliable and valid psychology.

PSYCHOLOGY DEFINED

Rudolph Goclenius, a Greek philosopher, invented the term 'psychology' in1590.

The English word 'Psychology' originated from the root 'psyche' in Greek. The root word in Greek meant 'soul' or 'spirit'. Logos in Greek meant 'knowledge.' Since the beginning psychology has been continuously undergoing redefinitions. Thus psychology was conceived to be a study of soul in the ancient time. At the end of the last century, psychology was recognized

as the study of mind and consciousness through
introspection, the description of experience. In 1818 James R. Angell, (J.B.Watson's professor) noted the pressure to shift the focus of psychology from consciousness to behavior moderated the position by defining behavior as "thinking, feeling and acting."

In the second decade of the century when extreme behaviorist stance arose and concept of consciousness was challenged and in 1913, John B. Watson defined psychology entirely in behavioral terms "the science of behavior." At the end of this century, the focus of psychology has been broadened and it is considered a science and practice concerned with human behavior as well as the mental processes that underlie physical and mental health. During the 1920s and 1930s, definitions in psychology dropped references to "mind" and "consciousness." In practice the subject of introspection largely disappeared by the 1930s. Howard C. Warren (1934), in his Dictionary of Psychology, gave four definitions of psychology, ranging from "a branch of science that investigates mental phenomena or mental operations" to "the science concerned with the mutual interrelations of organism and environment through transmission of energy," to "the systematic investigation of the behavior of organisms" to "the science of the self or personal individual." Norman Munn (1946) defined psychology as "the science of experience and behavior." In the late 1960s, cognitive psychology ushered and humanistic psychology gained popularity and the definition of psychology had a renewed emphasis on experience. By the 1970s, psychology's definition shifted yet again toward a more moderate and commonly defined "science of behavior and experience." In the last two decades of the century, the recognition that psychology is not only a science but also a practice. Currently, psychology is most often defined as "the study of behavior and underlying mental phenomena."

One of the philosophers sarcastically commented on this turn of events in which the terms soul, mind and consciousness were banished one by one in preference to the term behavior, that 'Psychology lost its soul first, its mind next, its consciousness later and is left to loath only with behavior.' Now, the extremism in psychology has subsided and psychologists are more tolerant and open to accept phenomena for their psychological enquiry including consciousness. Currently there is consensus among psychologists in defining psychology as *the study of behavior and mental processes (Coon and Mittrer, 2007).* Another definition made by other contemporary psychologists states, *"Psychology as the scientific study of behavior and mind (Passer and Smith, 2007).*

The subject matter of Psychology revolves around the study of behavior, human and animal. Psychology does not restrict itself to studying overt or observable behavior.
Overt behavior includes walking, talking, laughing, hitting, or jumping. It necessarily
includes study of covert behavior as well. Covert behavior includes internal events like learning, motivation, attitudes, beliefs, values, and feeling. Psychology is a Scientific Study. It involves systematic study of behavior and mental processes in which the observed data is organized based on theory. Further it involves measurement. Psychology is regarded a social science.

SCOPE OF PSYCHOLOGY
. The scope of psychology constantly extends to include a wide range of phenomena of scientific interest. The interest of the investigators ranges from interest in astrology, graphology to parapsychology. The psychological studies range from investigations of individuals to studies of groups, organizations and nations. Psychology studies all sorts of individuals, from mentally retarded to genius, from mentally ill to people who are selfactualizing. The spectrum of phenomena of interest to psychologists include every thing from egotism to altruism, from truancy, delinquency, criminality, psychopath to spiritualism, from peace to violence, terrorism and war, from behavior of plants to that of animals and human beings, and what not? It is not surprising that modern psychology has been some times commented to be a *psychotic octopus* that stretches and catches every thing that comes across

it by its innumerous ever lengthening limbs.

FIELDS OF PSYCHOLOGY

Psychology is a broadening and diversifying field. A number of different sub fields and specialty areas have newly emerged. The following are a few of the major areas of research and application within the field of psychology.

Clinical Psychology is the branch of psychology that is devoted to study, diagnosis and treatment abnormal behavior. Their area of work covers a large range from milder disturbances like adjustment disorders that occur due to identifiable stressor on one hand to the more severe disorders like schizophrenia where the level of impairment of psychological functioning in the individual is extreme. Learning about the factors contributing to clinically significant impairment or disorders, arriving at a diagnosis, and evolving methods to treat these disorders are the common interests of clinical psychologists. Some clinical psychologists devote all their time in applying the theoretical understanding on psychopathology to treat their clients who are called as practitioners. Some others are primarily interested in issues like delineating factors influencing mental breakdowns, identifying the first signs of psychiatric breakdowns, the efficacy of certain kinds of therapy on certain types of patients, etc. They carry out research on various aspects of psychopathology and are called as clinical researchers.

Community Psychology A related field to clinical psychology is the community psychology. Community psychology is a growing field that focuses on promoting community-wide mental health through research, prevention, education, and consultation.

Industrial and organizational psychology is also known as I/O psychology, work psychology, work and organizational psychology, W-O psychology, occupational personnel psychology or talent assessment. It is concerned with the application of psychological theories, research methods, and intervention strategies to solve workplace issues. I/O psychologists are interested in making organizations more productive and ensuring workers are able to lead physically and psychologically healthy lives. I/O psychologists are educated in the topics that include personnel psychology,motivation and leadership, employee selection, training and development, organization development and guided change, organizational behavior, and work and family issues. I/O psychologists who work in an organization are likely to work in the Human Resorce (HR) department. Many I/O psychologists pursue careers as independent consultants or applied academic researchers

.Consumer psychology is a branch related to Industrial-Organizational psychology.
It deals with issues like people's buying behavior, effects of advertisements on buying behavior, and better marketing strategies.

Health psychology investigates the relationship between psychological factors and physical illnesses. For example, they may be interested to study effect of psychological factors like maternal deprivation on physical illnesses like asthma. They also are interested in identifying health-enhancing behaviors like dieting, exercise, yoga on physical health and psychological well being, and promoting them among people. Further they research to identify psychological factors associated with health compromising behaviors like smoking, drinking. In addition to this they also work with those patients suffering from chronic or terminal illnesses, like diabetes and cancer, to evolve methods to rehabilitate them.

Medical Psychology is the field of psychology that applies psychology to manage medical problems. Issues like emotional impact of illness, self-screening for cancer and disabilities, and compliance in taking medications are within the scope of medical psychology.

Counseling psychology tries to study problems relating to educational, social and career adjustment. Health psychologists handle less severe problems than those attended to by the clinical psychologists. They teach students methods to enhance their learning capacity, helping the students to resolve their everyday difficulties, teaching the students principles to solve the problems with their roommates, etc. are done by counseling psychologists. Counseling psychologists employed in business organizations help the employees handle their problems that are work-related, interpersonal problems among colleagues, etc. Couples with marital problems also can seek help from counseling psychologists. Counselors also can help people handle their problems within the context of the family, like parents' difficulty in communicating with their children.

School Psychology is the branch of psychology that works within the educational system to help children with emotional, social, and academic issues. As a branch of psychology it applies principles of cinical psychology and educational psychology to the diagnosis and treatment of students' behavioral and learning problems. School psychologists are educated in child and adolescent development, learning, pychoeducational assessment, personality, therapeutic interventions, special education, sychology, consultation, child and adolescent psychpathology, etc., They help children and youth succeed academically, socially, and emotionally. They collaborate with educators, parents, and other professionals to create safe, healthy, and supportive learning environments for all children and to strengthen connections between home and school.

Industrial and organizational psychology is also known as I/O psychology, work psychology, work and organizational psychology, W-O psychology, occupational psychology, personnel psychology or talent assessment. It is concerned with the application of psychological theories, research methods, and intervention strategies to solve workplace issues. I/O psychologists are interested in making organizations more productive and ensuring workers are able to lead physically and psychologically healthy lives. I/O psychologists are educated in the topics that include personnel psychology,motivation and leadership, employee selection, training and development, organization development and guided change, organizational behavior, and work and family issues. I/O psychologists who work in an organization are likely to work in the Human Resorce (HR) department. Many I/O psychologists pursue careers as independent consultants or applied academic researchers

Consumer psychology, a branch related to Industrial-Organizational psychology, deals with issues like people's buying behavior, effects of advertisements on buying behavior, and better marketing strategies.

Engineering psychology focuses on ways to improve the relationship between people and machines. They design machines in such a manner as to reduce human error.

Some examples of the works of engineering psychologists are designing air traffic control systems and underwater habitats for oceanographic research. The design of the person-machine interface, the point at which the person interacts with the machine is especially important in computer systems.

Biopsychology specializes in understanding the biological bases of behavior. The field of Biopsychology focuses on the functions of the brain and nervous system. Studying about the various lobar functions and how neurotransmitters in our brains influence our behavior can be seen as some of the interests of Biopsychologists.

Comparative psychology is yet another field of psychology that has a fairly long history. It primarily focused on studying and comparing the behavior of different species, especially that of animals.

Experimental Psychology f o c us on the study of processes like sensation, perceiving, learning and thinking. If one is interested in finding out how one perceives pain, or how one learns new concepts the he would resort to experimental psychology.

Some critics question the term 'experimental psychology' as psychologists studying any other phenomena as well may use experimental method. Neither do the experimental psychologists limit themselves to purely experimental method of investigation.

Sensation and Perception Psychology deals with studies on the sense organs and the process of perception. It also is involved in investigating the mechanisms of sensation and developing theories about how perception occurs.

Learning psychology is related to studying about how and why learning occurs.
They invest large part of their work in attempts to develop theories of learning.

Cognitive psychology can be seen as a specialty that grew out of experimental psychology. It includes study of higher mental processes like thinking, language, memory, reasoning and logic, problem solving, and decision- making. In short, it deals with studying phenomena of human thinking and information processing.

Developmental psychology traces the behavioral changes that occur in people from years as prenatal stages to old age. They also study about the influence on the individual from the point of conception unto death and analyze how behavior is influenced by these varied factors. In short Developmental Psychologists deal with studying how people grow and change throughout the course of the lives. They are more concerned about universal milestones rather than focusing on individual changes.

Personality psychology This is the branch of psychology that focuses on individual differences is called. Both consistency in an individual's behavior and the changes occurring in him over time are points of interest to personality psychologists. In addition to this they try to understand how one individual is different from the other given the same situation, there by highlighting the uniqueness of the person.

Sports psychology If one is unable to carry on with his routine activities or if he is experiences difficulty in mixing with others around him then he would find it worthwhile to consult one of the psychologists who devote their effort in studying issues relating to physical and mental health.

Social psychology Man is a social animal. We are not isolated being. We are all parts of a complex network of social relationships. Social psychology studies how others affect people's thinking, feelings and behavior. Social psychologists cover various topics like how one forms attitude and prejudices, human aggression, decision making while in a group, and why we form relationships with others. Researches on difference between males and females, the acquisition of gender identity, and how gender affects behavior throughout one's life are of interest to the **gender psychologists**.

Cross-cultural psychology is a branch of psychology that deals w i t h investigating the similarities and differences in psychological functioning among various cultural and ethnic groups. This branch focuses on issues like how child-rearing practices differ with regard to different cultures, what are the factors affecting the achievement of women in different cultures, and why do cultures vary in their standards for physical attractiveness. Contemporary psychology invests a lot on studying the cultural diversity of virtually every psychological phenomenon.

Environmental psychology The numbers of specialty areas continue to grow even today. Environmental psychology is a field of psychology that studies the relationship between people and their physical environment. They study the effect of neighborhood, crowding, pollution and other environmental factors on psychological - factors like our social behavior, our emotions, perception of stress and even the way we think.

Forensic psychology deals with legal issues like deciding what criteria indicate that a person is legally insane, and whether smaller or larger juries make fairer decisions.

Space Psychology With more human beings visiting outer space than before the requirement of Space Psychology has come to be acknowledged. Space flights are longer and more frequent than earlier. This necessitated the emergence field of psychology that focuses on issues like screening of astronauts to weed out people who are more vulnerable to conflict in cramped, public quarters, handling the problem of space sickness, factors that affect sanity of crew that are on long space travels, decision making while on space travel when individuals are in small isolated groups, and so on.

METHODES IN PSYCHOLOGY:
INTROSPECTION:

- [ ] Look inside
- [ ] Look inward
- [ ] Self-perception
- [ ] Self-analysis
- [ ] Inner observation
- [ ] Self-observation

OBSERVATION:

- [ ] Participative
- [ ] Non participative

EXPRIMENTER METHODE:

- [ ] Control single group
- [ ] Control group design
- [ ] Multiple group design
- [ ] Rotating design

CLINICAL METHODE
PSYCHO PHYSICAL METHODE
STSTESTICAL/SURVEY METHODE

FIELDS OF SPECALISATION:

- [ ] Labour welfare
- [ ] Correctional social work
- [ ] Community development/social action/NGOs
- [ ] Social action
- [ ] Social welfare administration
- [ ] Medical/psychiatric setting

☐   Education/social work

UNIT – II
Life span – physical, social and psychological aspects of development from prenatal period to old age. Motivation and hierarchy of needs.

Growth development

Development – Task

Developmental stage – Life span

Studying of human development from child to old is called developmental psychology

Study of human development from conception to old age is called developmental psychology:

- Pre – natal period (0 – 270 days/10 months)
- Infant period - birth to 2nd weak
- Babyhood – 2nd weak to 2nd year
- Early childhood – 2 to 6 year
- Late childhood – 6 to 11 year
- Puberty – 11 to 14
- Adolescence – 14 to 18
- Early adulthood – 18 to 40
- Middle age – 40 to 60
- Old age – above 60

Malow's Theory of Need Hierarchy

Taking the clue from the observation that monkeys show a definite priority for satisfaction of their needs, Maslow conceived *the hierarchy of needs* involving five

broader layers staked on one after the other. These layers include, the physiological needs, the needs for safety and security, the needs for love and belonging, the needs for esteem, and the need to actualize the self, in that order, as may be seen in figure below.

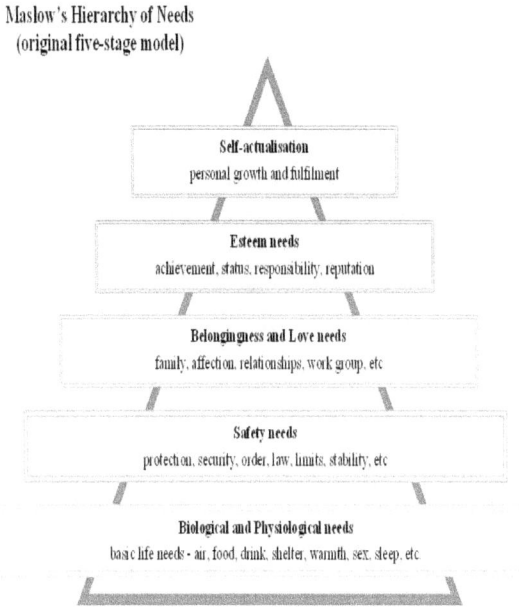

Maslow's Hierarchy of Needs
(original five-stage model)

Self-actualisation
personal growth and fulfilment

Esteem needs
achievement, status, responsibility, reputation

Belongingness and Love needs
family, affection, relationships, work group, etc

Safety needs
protection, security, order, law, limits, stability, etc

Biological and Physiological needs
basic life needs - air, food, drink, shelter, warmth, sex, sleep, etc

© alan chapman 2001-4, based on Maslow's Hierarchy of Needs

Not to be sold or published. More free online training resources are at www.businessballs.com. Alan Chapman accepts no liability.

The physiological needs include the needs to have for oxygen, water, protein, salt, sugar, calcium, and other minerals and vitamins, homeostasis, activity, rest, sleep, elimination of wastes, avoid pain and sex. Deprivation of such needs may drive the human being or the animal to go in pursuit of things that might satiate the needs. When the physiological needs are largely taken care of, *the safety and security needs* in the second layer of needs comes into play. Under such condition an individual will become increasingly interested in finding safe circumstances, stability, protection and develop a need for structure, for order, some limits.

When physiological needs and safety needs are, by and large, taken care of, *the love and belonging needs* in the third layer starts to show up. One may begin to feel the need for friends, a sweetheart, children, affectionate relationships in general, even a sense of community. When the love and belonging needs are met one move towards *the esteem needs.* The esteem needs may be either lower or higher. The lower one is the need for the respect of others, the need for status, fame, glory, recognition, attention, reputation, appreciation, dignity, even dominance and the higher form involves the need for self-respect, including such feelings as confidence, competence, achievement, mastery, independence, and freedom.

The preceding four levels of needs are called *deficit needs*, or *D-needs*. If one doesn't have enough of something and has a deficit he feels the need. But if one get all he or she needs, he or she feels nothing at all. Such need satisfaction cease to be motivating.

He also talks about these levels in terms of *homeostasis.* When body, lacks a certain substance, it develops a hunger for it and when it gets enough of it, then the hunger stops. Thus the homeostatic principle could be extended to such needs as safety, belonging, and esteem that we don't ordinarily think of in these terms. All these needs are essentially survival needs. Even love and esteem are needed for the maintenance of health and we all have these needs built in to us genetically, like instincts. They are hence called *instinctoid,* instinct- like needs.

Self-actualization

The last level of needs in the need hierarch is called growth *motivation.* The needs in the last layer stand in contrast to D-motivation and hence are essentially called *B-needs.* The B- needs and D -needs are also termed being needs and becoming needs respectively. These are the needs that do not involve balance or homeostasis. Once engaged, they continue to be felt and they are likely to become stronger as one starts feeling them. These needs involve the continuous desire to fulfill self potentials and to "be all that one can be." They are the needs for *self-actualization.*

Self Actualizes

Maslow has identified the personality of self actualizes using *biographical analysis.* He analyzed the biographies of a group of selected individuals who represented self-actualization in their life. The group of individuals selected for the analysis include Abraham Lincoln, Thomas Jefferson, Albert Einstein, Eleanor Roosevelt, Jane Adams, William James, Albert Schweitzer, Benedict Spinoza, and Alduous Huxley, and 12

unnamed people who were alive at the time. The self-actualizers were *reality-centered,* in that they usually differentiated between what is fake and dishonest from what is real and genuine. T h e y were *problem-centered,* in that they treated life's difficulties as problems demanding solutions, not as personal troubles to be railed at or surrendered to.

They had a *different perception of means and ends.* They felt that the ends don't necessarily justify the means, that the means could be ends themselves, and that the journey was often more important than the ends.

The self-actualizers also had a different way of relating to others in that they enjoyed *solitude,* and were comfortable being alone. They enjoyed deeper *personal relations* with a few close friends and family members, rather than more shallow relationships with many. They enjoyed *autonomy,* a relative independence from physical and social needs, and they resisted *enculturation,* in that they were not susceptible to social pressure to be "well adjusted" or to "fit in." They were nonconformists in the best sense of the term. They had an *unhostile sense of humor,* preferring to joke at their own expense, or at the human condition, and never directing their humor at others. They showed an *acceptance of self and others,* by which he meant that these people would be more likely to take any one as he or she is than try to change him or her into what they thought he or she should be. They applied the same acceptance to their attitudes towards themselves as well. They were often strongly motivated to change negative qualities in themselves that could be changed, and if some quality of theirs wasn't harmful, they let it be, even enjoying it as a personal quirk. They were given to *spontaneity and simplicity. .*

They preferred being themselves rather than being pretentious or artificial, But, for all their nonconformity they seem to be committed, they tended to be conventional on the surface rather be dramatic. They had a sense of *humility and respect* towards others. They *democratic values* in that they were open to ethnic and individual variety, even treasuring it. They had a quality called Gemeinschaftsgefühl , *human kinship that connotes* social interest, compassion, humanity. This was accompanied by a *strong ethics,* which was spiritual but seldom conventionally religious in nature. They had a certain *freshness of appreciation,* an ability to see things, even ordinary things, with wonder and also ability t o b e *creative,* inventive, and original. Finally, they tended to have more *peak*

experiences than the average person. Such peak experience involves an experience in which one transcends himself or herself and feels being very tiny, or very large, to some extent one with life or nature or God. Peak experience installs in a person a feeling of being a part of the infinite and the eternal. The peak experiences tend to leave their mark on a person, change them for the better, and many actively seek them out. The peak experiences are also called mystical experiences. They are an important part of many religious and philosophical traditions. Self-actualizers were not perfect human beings.

They often suffered considerable anxiety and guilt, but, which were realistic rather than misplaced or neurotic ones. Some of them were absentminded and overly kind and some of them had unexpected moments of ruthlessness, surgical coldness, and loss of humor.

Two other points he makes about these self-actualizers: Their values were "natural" and seemed to flow effortlessly from their personalities. And they appeared to transcend many of the dichotomies others accept as being undeniable, such as the differences between the spiritual and the physical, the selfish and the unselfish, and the masculine and the feminine.

Metaneeds and metapathologies

The special, driving needs (B-needs,) of the self-actualizers distinguishes them from others. The B-needs needed for the self-actualizers in their lives in order to be happy include truth, goodness, beauty, goodness, beauty, unity/wholeness/transcendence of opposites, aliveness, uniqueness, perfection and necessity, completion, justice and order, simplicity, richness, effortlessness, playfulness, self-sufficiency and meaningfulness. When a self-actualizer doesn't get these needs fulfilled, they respond with *metapathologies*. That is when forced to live without these values, the self-actualizers develop depression, despair, disgust, alienation, and a degree of cynicism.

UNIT – III

Learning – meaning – theory of learning – the classical conditioning – operant conditioning cognitive learning – methods of effective learning – nature of memory forgetting – thinking – perception – concept and types – perception and sensation – characteristics of perception laws and perception grouping – errors in perception.

LEARNING
INTRODUCTION

Learning is a process that depends on one's experience. It is something that results in long term changes in behavior potential. Many theories are available that provide a varied explanation on learning process. Major traditional behavioristic theories are classical conditioning, operant conditioning, observational learning and cognitive learning. These theories provide important insights into learning, even though some of them use much simpler organisms than humans to draw emperical evidences supporting their stand.

Pavlov's experiment with dogs, Skinner's experiment with rats and pigeons, Tolman's experiment with rats, and Kohler's experiments with chimps are few examples.This lesson will cover the basic theories of learning, specifically the behavioral and cognitive theories.

NATURE OF LEARNING

Learning is often referred to as a relatively permanent change in behavior (or behavior potential) that results from experience or practice. Changes in behavior due to maturation process or that occurs as a result of temporary conditions like effect of drug, adaptation, disease, and fatigue.

The phrase 'relatively permanent' in the definition above implies that changes in behavior that are transient or spontaneously reversible cannot be considered as learned behavior. For instance, adaptation to dim illumination can be easily reversed on exposure to bright light. Even repeated exposure to this process does not affect the nature of change. On the contrary, a behavior that is learned is long lasting and repeated exposure affects the nature of change. The change is accumulative.

For 'learning' to be inferred the change has to observable. It should be either directly observable from the way in which an individual behaves, or it should be indirectly observed by comparing those exposed to certain conditions with those who are denied the exposure.

The term 'due to practice' denotes exposure to specific experiences. Now consider the example of an experimental condition that studies verbal learning. Practice, here, would refer to successive presentation of list of words at a rate determined by the experimenter.

Imprinting and habituation may be eliminated from what it means by learning since neither of these phenomena involves practice. Similarly, short term memory would be excluded from what is considered as 'learning' because it is not a 'relatively permanent' change.

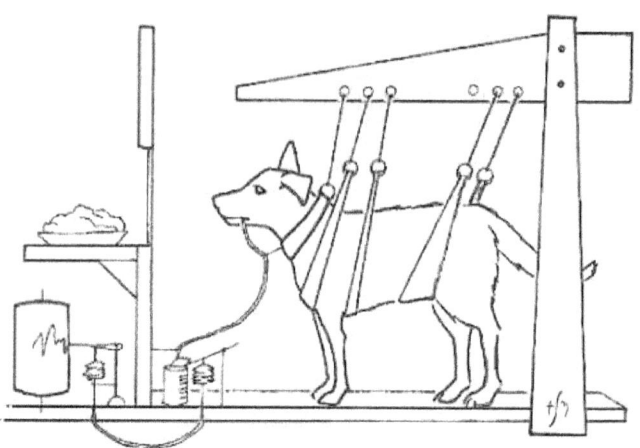

Though literally a number of different problems have been investigated by learning studies only a small number of paradigms are needed to describe the experimental procedures. Paradigms refer to the basic arrangements used by an experimenter to produce the phenomenon that is of interest to him. The few paradigms that have been used in experiments on learning are listed below:

· Classical Conditioning
· Operant Conditioning
· Observational Learning
· Cognitive Learning

CLASSICAL CONDITIONING

Russian Physiologist, Ivan Pavlov, is famous for his theory of classical conditioning. Conditioning is a process by which a natural response to a stimulus begins to follow another stimulus that remained neutral to it earlier. Pavlovian Classical Conditioning was considered as the prototype of all learning by most psychologists of the 1920s.

Pavlov's Experiment

Pavlov, while experimenting with dogs to study his physiological research, noticed that the dog salivated not only to the sight of food but also to the sound of footsteps of the attendant who brought food. The dogs were responding to both the biological need (hunger). In addition to this natural response they also displayed a learned response of salivating to a neutral stimulus 'footstep of the attendant'. This kind of learning is termed as 'Classical Conditioning'.

Classical conditioning is one in which an organism learns a response to a neutral stimulus that had not brought that response earlier. To demonstrate classical conditioning Pavlov conducted a series of experiments. For instance, in one of his experiments he attached a tube to the salivary gland of the dog that helped him to measure precisely the amount of salivation that occurred. Then, he sounded the bell few minutes after which he presented the dog with meat powder. While pairing the sound of bell and the presentation of meat powder Pavlov made sure that exactly the same amount of time lapsed between the presentation of sound and the meat. During the initial trials of the experiment the dog would salivated only to the meat powder. However, after few pairings of the sound and the meat the dog started salivating just on hearing the sound, even when there was no meat presented.

We would perhaps have a startle reaction when we hear a bell and would not salivate. It is obvious that salivation was not a natural response to the sounding of bell. Hence the sound of the bell in the experiment mentioned above is a **neutral stimulus**.

Salivating to the meat is a natural response. When meat is placed on the mouth of the dog it would salivate because of the biological makeup of the dog. Hence the meat in the above experiment is called the **unconditioned stimulus (US)** and the salivation produced in response to presentation of meat is an **unconditioned response (UR)**.

Unconditioned responses are innate responses that are natural and that do not involve any training. They are always a response to the unconditioned stimulus.

For conditioning to take place the neutral stimulus (ringing of bell) is repeatedly paired with unconditioned stimulus (meat powder). During the process of conditioning the bell gradually gets associated with the meat. Now the bell brings in the same kind of response like that of the meat. During this phase the salivation gradually increases each time the bell is sounded, until the bell alone in the absence of meat powder causes the dog to salivate.

By the time the conditioning is complete the bell has evolved from a neutral stimulus to a Conditioned Stimulus (CS). The bell, now, can bring in salivation on its own. Salivating to the bell is called as Conditioned Response (CR).

Extinction.

The property of the conditioned stimulus to bring in a conditioned brought out by conditioned response is not permanent. It gradually loses its property is it is presented alone without the unconditioned stimulus over a number of trails. This phenomenon is called as extinction. **Extinction** occurs when a previously conditioned response gradually decreases in frequency and disappears eventually in time.

Spontaneous Recovery

One interesting fact about conditioning is that once a conditioned response is extinguished it is not vanished forever. The extinguished response may reappear after time has elapsed without exposure to the conditioned stimulus. This is called **spontaneous recovery**. Nevertheless, the response that occurs after the extinction is much weaker that the original conditioned response and they would get extinguished more readily than before.

Stimulus Generalization

Pavlov noticed that his dogs that were used in conditioning were not only responding to the sound of the bell but also to stimulus that were similar to bell, like the sound of the buzzer, or the tuning fork. This phenomenon he termed as **stimulus generalization**. It occurs when a conditioned response follows a stimulus that is similar in characteristics to the original conditioned stimulus. The more the two stimuli are similar the greater would be the generalization.

Stimulus Discrimination

On the other hand, if the stimuli are sufficiently different from one another that they both are perceived as different then only the conditioned stimulus would evoke a conditioned response and the other would not. This is called **stimulus discrimination**. It is the process by which an organism learns to differentiate among stimuli and restricts its response to one stimulus in particular.

Higher-order conditioning

One conditioned stimulus can act as a natural stimulus when paired with a neutral stimulus. Such frequent pairing would get the organism respond to the neutral stimulus as it would to the conditioned stimulus. This is called **higher-order conditioning**. It is a form of conditioning that occurs when an already conditioned stimulus is paired with a neutral stimulus over a number of trials till such time the neutral stimulus evokes the same response as that of the conditioned stimulus.

The classical conditioning explains how we learn responses like fear for darkness and how one gets back to drinking at the sight of alcohol after a period of abstinence.

Much of our behavior in daily life can be explained using classical conditioning.

OPERANT CONDITIONING

Not all learning is involuntary. Operant conditioning explains how voluntary responses are strengthened or weakened depending on positive or negative consequences.

In classical conditioning the original behavior is a natural biological response. On the contrary, operant conditioning is applied on the behaviors that are voluntary. In operant conditioning the organism performs a behavior deliberately in order to produce a desirable outcome. Here the organism operates on its environment to produce a result that it desires.

Thorndike's Law of Effect

E.L.Thorndike observed that when cats were put in a cage with a fish dangling outside the cats would learn, by trial and error, to press the paddle and get out of the cage.

He explained this formulating the **Law of effects**. He theorized that responses that satisfy are more likely to be repeated while those that are not satisfying are less likely to be repeated. Here, in his experiment, pressing the paddle resulted in satisfaction since the cat could get out of the cage by this behavior. Hence the cat learnt the response of pressing the paddle that it tends to repeat every time it was put in the cage.

Picture courtesy: http://www.animalbehaviour.net/OperantConditioning.htm **7.4.2**
Skinner's Experiment

14

Thorndike's research served as the foundation for the work of B.F.Skinner who is considered to be one among the most popular behaviorists of his times. Skinner devised a Skinner box that he used to study operant conditioning. The animals in the Skinner box learn to press the lever so as to obtain food that would be delivered on the tray placed inside the box.

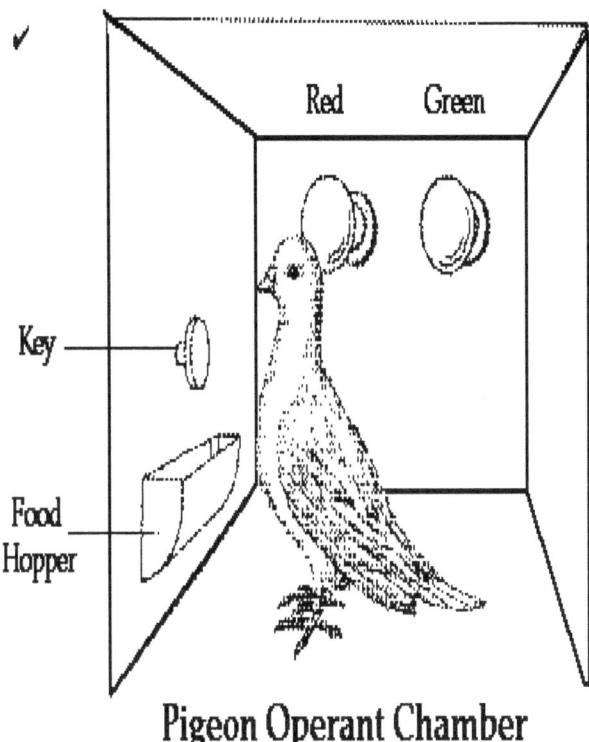

Pigeon Operant Chamber

Suppose a pigeon is placed inside the **Skinner box**. It would just move around exploring the place in a relatively random fashion. By chance, at some point of time, it would peck the key that in turn would result in delivery of food pellet. The pigeon does not learn the connection between the pecking at the hole key and getting the food pellet right after the first trial. It would still continue exploring the box. Again by chance, sooner or later, the pigeon pecks the key and gets the food pellet delivered. In time the frequency of the pecking behavior will increase. Eventually the pigeon would simple go pecking the key to get the food pellets until its hunger is satisfied. This demonstrates that the pigeon has learnt that receipt of food pellet is contingent on the pecking behavior.

The pigeons in a variation of this experiment were taught to discriminate between two stimuli using the same principle of reinforcement. As seen in the picture above the Skinner Box was provided with two lights (red and green). If the pigeons pecked the key when green light was on then it was provided with a food pellet. On the other hand if it pecked the key when red light was on the pigeon will not get any food pellet. The red and green lights were randomly flashed for brief periods in the experiment. The pigeons gradually learned to discriminate between red light and green light. They pecked the key only when the green light was on and not when the red light was on!

Types of Reinforcement

In this situation, the food pellet serves as a reinforcer that increases the probability that the pecking behavior will be repeated. Any stimulus that increases the probability of occurrence of a preceding behavior is termed as a reinforcer. There are two types of rein forcers: the primary reinforcer and the secondary reinforcer.

Primary reinforcer and Secondary reinforcer. A primary reinforcer is that stimulus that satisfies biological needs like hunger and thirst. Food to satisfy hunger, water to satisfy thirst, and woolen clothes to keep oneself warm can be seen as primary reinforcers. In contrast, a **secondary reinforcer** becomes reinforcing not by itself, but because of its association with the primary reinforcer. Money is a reinforcer because it can get us food, or a bottle of biseleri water. What makes a stimulus a reinforcer is highly individualistic. If on presentation of the stimulus the rate of response of previously occurring behavior increases then that stimulus can be identified as a reinforcer.

Positive reinforcer. Another way in which reinforcers are classified is based on their effect on behavior. If a reinforcer increases the probability of occurrence of a behavior then it is termed as positive reinforcer. Food, water, praise, and money, for example, when presented following a response are likely to increase the likelihood of occurrence of the response in future. These are examples of positive reinforcers.

Negative reinforcer. On the contrary, if removal of a stimulus following a response results in increased probability of occurrence of the behavior then it is a negative reinforcer. A typical example is going to a movie when you are worked out to relieve your tension. In this example getting rid of your tensions and getting refreshed after a movie reinforces movie-going behavior. Removal of the negative state increases the occurrence of the behavior, and this acts as negative reinforcer.

Punishment. Punishment is presenting a negative stimulus that would decrease the occurrence of the behavior. The distinction between negative reinforcement and punishment is very important. While negative reinforcement involves removing of negative stimulus punishment involves presenting a negative stimulus. Negative reinforcement increases the occurrence of the behavior while punishment decreases the occurrence of the behavior.

Schedules of reinforcement

Equally important as the type of reinforcement is the schedule of reinforcement.

The frequency and the timing of reinforcement following the behavior are varied in different schedules of reinforcement. Continuous reinforcement is one where every time the organism exhibits the desired behavior it is reinforced. For example, a pigeon on continuous reinforcement schedule would get a food pellet every time it pecks the key.

The other type of reinforcement schedule is called the partial reinforcement schedule. In this schedule the behavior is reinforced some, and not all, of the times. Gambling is a typical example of partial reinforcement. In this the behavior may some times be rewarded and some times not.

Although many different partial reinforcement have been studied four of them are popularly used. The schedules differ in two ways: one is the number of responses needed to elicit reinforcement, and the other is the amount of time that needs to be elapsed before the reinforcement. The first type may be of either fixed-ratio or variable-ratio schedule.

The second type may be of either fixed- interval or variable- interval schedule.

Fixed-Ratio schedule. In the fixed-ratio schedule the reinforcement is provided only after a certain number of responses made. Piece-rate pay in industry is a typical example of this. A tailor in an industry will receive the pay depending on the number of garments she has stitched. Another example is a pigeon on a FR10 schedule would receive a food pellet after every 10th peck.

Variable-Ratio Schedule. On the contrary, in variable-ratio schedule reinforcement is provided after an average number of responses but unpredictably.

Gambling devices and systems that arrange occasional but unpredictable payoffs may be seen as examples of this type of reinforcement. Another example of this could be a pigeon on VR10 that would receive food pellet after say 5th, 10th, 9th, 15th, 11th over five trails which averages out to 10 (5+10+9+15+11=50, and average rate of reinforcement would be 50/5=10).

Fixed-Interval schedule. This type of schedule is one in which the organism is reinforced after an established time interval. For example, a rat on FI 5 may be reinforced once every five minutes. The major drawback of this schedule is that the behavior decreases immediately after reinforcement. The rat would stop responding immediately after reinforcement but responds more and more rapidly as the time for the next reinforcement approaches.

Variable-interval schedule. In this schedule the reinforcement is given at various times, and it generally results in more consistent behavior. If a response has been reinforced on the average every five minutes but unpredictably, the rat responds at a steady rate. For example, a rat on VI 10 would receive reinforcement after say 7th, 12th, 10th, 10th, 11th second (7+12+10+10+11=50, and average rate of reinforcement would be 50/5=10). The rate is high if the average interval is short, and the rate is low if it is long.

OBSERVATIONAL LEARNING

Conditioning principles do not exhaust possible explanations of all behaviors, especially human learning. Learning need not occur through direct experience.

Observational learning, in which we observe and imitate others behaviors, also play a big part. The process of observing and imitating specific behavior is often called modeling.

By observing and imitating models we learn all kinds of social behaviors. Bandura and others (1961) have developed their social learning based on social modeling.

Principles of Observational Learning

This type of learning was first explained by Albert Bandura (1977) in his popular social learning theory. He says we learn by watching others. People whose behavior is observed are called Models. Any one can serve as a model. Examples of models can be parents, politician, movie stars, friends or even the boy next door. If the model's behavior is rewarded then the observer may imitate that behavior. On the other hand, if the model's behavior is not rewarded one may not imitate that behavior.

Bobo Doll Experiment

The observational learning was dramatically demonstrated by Bandura and his coworkers. In the classic experiment by Bandura young children watched a film of an adult wildly hitting a 5- foot-tall inflated bobo doll (Bandura, Ross, & Ross, 1963a, 1963b).

Later the children were brought to another room where attractive toys were kept but were

FIGURE 2.3 Photographs of children imitating the aggressive behavior of the female model they had observed on film. (Bandura, Ross, and Ross, 1963a)

denied the chance to play with the attractive toys. This was done to frustrate the children since the experimenters were interested to see the children's reaction to frustration. The children were now given the bobo dolls similar to the one shown on the movie, and sure enough the children displayed the same kind of behavior as it was done by adult models in the movies. Amazingly some of the children mimicked the aggressive behavior almost identically. The complete sequence of Bandura's experiment is shown in the picture below.

Not only negative behaviors but also positive behaviors are learned through observational learning. When children were exposed to a model playing with a dog in 'Fearless Peer' they were more likely to approach a strange dog than those children who had not watches the Fearless Peer.

Steps in Observational Learning

According to Bandura, observational learning takes place through four steps. The first step involves paying attention to the model's behavior. Attention is drawn towards a modeled behavior and most critical feature of the model's behavior is noted. After doing so the mental image of the model's behavior is stored in memory so that it can be retrieved later. The third step involves reproducing the action. Any specific situation similar to the one stored in memory may trigger us to convert remembered behavior into action. The fourth step involves remaining motivated to learn and carry out the behavior.

If the action performed by us is reinforced we add it to our behavior repertoire or else it may be gradually wither away.

COGNITIVE LEARNING

The cognitive learning theorists argue that learning cannot be reduced to mere forming of 'association' as contented by Pavlovian and Skinnerian psychologists. They hold that cognitive process like perception, thinking and memory play key role in learning. Insight Learning by Kohler and Latent Learning by Tolman may be seen as examples of cognitive learning theories. In fact even Bandura's observational learning may be seen as an instance of cognitive learning since it also explains learning as one that involves attention, imagery, and memory. In sum, the cognitive learning theorists try to study the cognitive processes that underlie learning. Cognitive learning connotes higher-level learning involving knowing, understanding, and anticipation.

Insight Learning.

Wolfgang Kohler, German psychologist, proposed that sudden recognition of relationships lead to solution of complex problem. He experimented with chimpanzees.

Kohler's work with chimpanzees, carried out in 1920's, remains particularly important to understand cognitive learning. The problems that Kohler set for his chimpanzees left enough scope for insight, because no parts of the problem were hidden from view(in contrast to Skinnerian experiments where the food dispenser in skinner box are hidden from the animal's view). Typically Kohler placed a chimpanzee in an enclosed area with a desirable piece of fruit, often banana, out of reach. To obtain the fruit the animal had to use the near by object as a tool. Usually the chimpanzee solved the problem, and did it in a way that suggested he had some insight.

Kohler's Experiment with Sultan. Kohler's typical experiment can be described as follows: Sultan [Kohler's most intelligent chimpanzee] is squatting at the bars but cannot reach the fruit which lies outside by means of his only available short stick. A longer stick is placed outside the bars about two meters on one side of the object and parallel with the grating. It cannot be grasped with the hand, but it can be pulled within reach by means of small stick. Sultan tries to reach the fruit with the smaller of two sticks. Not succeeding, he tears at a piece of wire that projects from the netted cage, but that is too in vain. Then he gazes about him (there are always in the course of these tests some long pauses, during which the animal scrutinizes the whole visible area). He suddenly picks up the little stick once again, goes upto the bars directly opposite to the long stick, pulls it towards him with the "auxiliary", seizes it, and goes with it to the point opposite to the objective (the fruit), which he secures.

Several aspects of the performance of those chimpanzees are unlike those of Thorndike's cat on skinner's rats and pigeons. The solution here is sudden rather than being the result of a gradual trial and error process. Another point is that once a chimpanzee solved a problem with few irrelevant moves. This is most unlike a rat, which continues to make irrelevant responses in Skinner box for many trials. Kohler's chimpanzees could readily transfer what they have learned to a novel situation. For example in one problem, sultan was not put in a cage, but some bananas were placed too high for him reach. To solve the problem, sultan stacked some boxes thrown around him, claimed the "platform", and grabbed the bananas. In subsequent problems, if the fruit was again too high to reach, sultan found other objects to construct a platform. In some cases sultan used table and a small ladder, and in one case sultan pulled Kohler himself over and used the experimenter as a platform.

Critical aspects of Insight Learning. There are three critical aspects of the chimpanzee's solution: its suddenness, its availability once discovered and its transferability. These aspects are at odds with the behaviorist notion of trial and error behaviors like the one observed by Thorndike, Skinner, and others. Instead the chimpanzee's solution may reflect a mental trial and error. The animal forms a mental representation until it hits on a solution, and then enacts the solution in the real world.

The solution, therefore, appears sudden because the representation persists over time, and the solution is transferable because the representation is either abstract enough to cover more than the original situation or malleable enough to be extended to a novel situation.

Cognitions in Animals. More recent studies done on primates provide even stronger evidence for cognition in animal learning. Particularly fascinating are studies showing that chimpanzees can acquire abstract concepts that were once believed to be the sole province of humans. In the typical study, chimpanzees learn to use plastic tokens of different shapes size and colors as words. For example, they might learn one token refers to apple and another to papers, where there is no physical resemblance between the token and the object. The fact that chimpanzees can learn these references means they understand concrete concept like "apple" and "paper". More impressively they also have abstract concept like "same", "different" and "cause". Thus chimpanzees can learn to use their "same" token when presented either two "apple" tokens or two "orange" ones and their "different" token when presented one "apple" and one "orange" token. Likewise chimpanzees seem to understand casual relations: they will apply token for "cause" when someone cut paper and scissors, but not when shown some intact paper and scissors (premack, 1985a; premack&premack, 1983).

Tolman's Sign Learning

Operant Conditioning principle emphasis that the reinforcement in essential to 'stamp in' new behavior. In contrast, latent learning principle suggests that learning occurs even in the absence of reinforcement. However, for the behavior to occur overtly reinforcement is requirement. It is for demonstration and not for learning per se that reinforcement is required. This is demonstrated by Edward Tolman. His experiments are said to demonstrate what is called Sign learning or latent learning.

The Pavlovian conditioning theorists believe that the rat learns specific units of S-R connections. The Skinnerian conditioning theorists believe that the rat learns the situation through successive approximations that is shaping, and perhaps, chaining.

However Tolman believes that the exact thing that happens in the learning is signs and not the learning of specific units either alone or in combination and summation. The rat rather learns a cognitive map of learning task. Sign learning connotes an acquired expectation that one stimulus will be followed by another in a particular context. Thus, what is learned is expectations rather than sequence of responses. Tolman allowed his rats to learn a maze and later interrupted their path with barriers. The rats immediately shifted to the nearest straight path to their goal as if they already knew the entire path.

Even when the maze has been suddenly rotated to 90°, the rats were able to follow their learned path. These experiments, Tolman holds show that the learning occurring in these cases are sign learning not mere bonding of unitary S-Rs.

Tolman's classic experiment. Tolman's classic experiment demonstrating latent learning consisted of three groups of rats that were made to run in complex maze for 16 consecutive days. Rats in Group 1 i.e., 'Reward group' were rewarded every time they reached goal box on all the 16 days. Rats in Group 2 i.e., in 'Non-reward group' were not given any reward on any of 16 days when they it reached goal box. The rats in the Group 3 i.e., 'Latent Learning group' were not given any reward for the first 10 days, but were given reward for the remaining 6 days. Results of Tolman's experiment were interesting.

For the first 10 days the rats in the Reward groups did better than those in the Non-reward and Latent Learning groups. On the 11th day when the reward was introduced for the first time to the rats in the Latent Learning group they performed as well as the ones in the Reward group.

This demonstrates the distinction between learning and performance.
Cognitive maps are internal images or mental representations of an area like maze, city, campus, and the like that underlie an ability to choose alternative paths to the same goals. The rats seemed to develop a 'Cognitive Map' of maze even when no reward was given. When reward was administered to them this cognitive map allowed them to reach high level of performance immediately.

Discovery learning is a type of cognitive learning in which skills are gained by insight and understanding and not by rote (de Jong & Van Joolingen, 1998). Although rote learning is efficient most psychologists agree that when people discover facts and principles on their own then it is more lasting and flexible than rote learning. Discovery seems to offer better understanding of new and unusual problems. Two groups of students, for instance, were asked to calculate the area of a parallelogram by multiplying the height by the length of the base. One group was encouraged to see how a piece of parallelogram could be moved to create a rectangle. Later both the groups of students were made to work on problems where height times base formula didn't seem to work.

Those students who simply memorized the formula got confused. Those who were encouraged to discover had better understanding of this new problem. Thus the best teaching strategies are based on guided discovery where in the students are given adequate freedom to actively think about problems and adequate guidance to gain useful knowledge by themselves.

FORGETTING

Forgetting or retention loss connotes the apparent loss of information already encoded and stored in an individual's long term memory. It can be a spontaneous one or may involve a gradual process in which old memories are unable to be recalled. There are many reasons why we forget things. Some of them are briefly discussed below.

Causes of Forgetting

There are five basic reasons for why forgetting occurs:

1) The decay of memory trace,
2) Problems with interfering materials,
3) A break down in retrieval process,
4) Emotional and motivational conditions, and
5) Organic factors

Decay of memory trace: This decay maybe said to occur due to neuro-chemical or anatomical changes. Some state that information in the STM may decay but that information in the LTM are permanent and difficulty in recalling events maybe due to retrieval problems. Some scientists state that decay does occur in the LTM and that memorized decay over time and disappear. If decay theory explained all forgetting, we would expect that the longer the time between the initial learning of information and our attempt to recall it, the harder it would be to remember it, since there would be more time for the memory trace to decay. Yet people who take several consecutive tests won the same material often recall more of the initial information when taking later tests than they did on earlier tests. If decay were operating we would expect the opposite to occur.

Interference mechanism: This theory states that our memory of new information maybe hindered by the events that occur before or after we learn. There may be two types of interference, Retroactive interference and Proactive interference.

INTERFERENCE
PROACTIVE INTERFERENCE
MARATHI IS IMPAIRED BY
MEMORY OF HINDI
LANGUAGE
HINDI
MARATHI
TEST
RETROACTIVE INHIBITION
HINDI IS IMPAIRED BY
MEMORY OF MARATHI

Retroactive interference occurs when a later event interferes with recall of earlier information. Proactive interference is where previously learnt information hinders learning in the present.

The following diagram illustrates experimental paradigm followed in experiments on retroactive and proactive interference.

Experimental Design for the study of Retroactive interference:
Group
Step 1
Step 2
Step 3
Experimental Group Learn Hindi
Learn Marathi
Test retention of Hindi
Control Group
Learn Hindi
Rest
Test retention of Hindi
Experimental design for the study of proactive interference
Group
Step 1
Step 2
Step 3
Experimental Group Learn Hindi
Learn Marathi
Test retention of Marathi
Control Group
Rest
Learn Marathi
Test retention of Marathi

Retrieval failure: In certain cases retrieval may not occur because of the TOT phenomenon. Failure to retrieve information does not mean the information has disappeared it may mean that there has been a poor encoding of the information. Even memories that seem impossible to retrieve may pop into mind when right cues are used.

Motivated forgetting: Repression is an example of motivated forgetting where memories that is painful, embarrassing or degrading maybe forcibly forgotten. According to Freud, repression occurs because we re unable to deal with these events in the conscious level. There is general agreement among psychologists that motivated forgetting dies play a role in blocking at least some material stored in long term memory.

Organic causes of forgetting: Certain physical illnesses or accidents may cause a loss of memory. There are three prominent types of organic amnesia: 1) Amnesia caused by disease
2) Retrograde Amnesia
3) Anterograde Amnesia

Amnesia caused by disease:
Some diseases produce actual physical
deterioration of brain cells, impairing memory as well as a variety of cognitive functions.

For instance, cardiovascular disease is characterized by decreased blood circulation, which sometimes limits o2 supply to the brain to the point that some brain cells die.

Strokes are another common physical cause of memory impairment. Here, a vessel in the brain ruptures, with resulting damage to cells. Alzheimer's disease is another illness that produces progressively widespread degeneration of brain cells. This devastating disease produces severe memory deficits and other impairments of mental functioning.
Retrograde Amnesia: Sometimes a blow to the head may cause loss of memory for certain details or events that occurred prior to the accidents. This condition is called as retrograde amnesia. In many of the cases, lost memories return gradually, with older memories tending to come back first. In almost all cases investigated, memories for recent events have been shown to be more susceptible to disruption than older memories. Retrograde amnesia is more likely to impair declarative memory, particularly episodic type, than to interfere with procedural memory
8.5.1.5.3

Anterograde Amnesia: Amnesia can also work in the opposite direction.
Some victims of brain damage may be able to recall old memories established before the damage but cannot remember information processed after the damage has occurred. This condition is called anterograde amnesia. It may be caused by injury to a specific area of the brain. It may also be associated with certain surgical procedure and chronic alcoholism. Unlike retrograde amnesia, anterograde amnesia is often irreversible.

PERCEPTION
INTRODUCTION
Our brain organizes and gives meaning to sensory inputs by the process called Perception. Perception includes process of selecting, ordering, synthesizing and interpreting the sensory impressions that impinge on our sensory organs. Studies on perception are focused to find out how we take the stimuli and form conscious representations of the environment around us.

Perception is an outgrowth of sensation. Sensation can be seen as the first encounter with a raw sensory stimulus. On the other hand, perception is a process by which the raw sensory impressions are interpreted, analyzed and integrated with other sensory information.

The basic principle of perceptual processing is selective attention. It refers to focusing on one or few stimuli of particular significance and ignoring the other stimuli. Sudden changes in the stimulus, contrast and novelty, extreme stimulus intensity like very high or very low intensity, repetition and difficult stimuli are few of the factors that affect our attention.
LAWS OF PERCEPTUAL ORGANIZATION
Our basic perceptual process works according to a series of principles referred to as gestalt laws of organization. The gestalt laws of organization were put forth by a group of German psychologists in early 1900s (Wertheimer, 1923) that is found to be valid for visual and auditory stimuli. These principles explain how bits and pieces of information are organized into meaningful wholes.

The elementary sensations that are usually in the form of dots, lines, edges, brightness, and varied hues are structured into the objects as seen by us because of this phenomenon called **perceptual organization**.

Among the various principles of perceptual organization the following are found to be very prominent:
1. Figure and Ground
2. Perceptual Grouping
3. Closure

Figure Ground

Processing and interpretation of information takes place in various levels as a result of perceptual organization. Figure-ground segregation is one aspect of perceptual organization. Imagine a visual stimulus that is a blob of contours at the retinal level. In this, the figure is an integrated group of contours while the ground is the background against which it stands. Often not all of its contours are actually detected at the retina when a figure is perceived. Some of them are subjective contours. These contours are not physically present at the retina, but are the product of intelligent perception.

Top-down processing is one where the perception is guided by knowledge, experience, expectations and motivations. Bottom- up processing is one that involves recognition and processing of information about individual components of a stimulus.

Hence, phenomenon of figure-ground segregation is not a purely bottom-up process (*i.e.* , it is not simply data-driven) but is bottom- up (data-driven) as well as top-down (conceptually-driven).

The above figure can either be seen a vase or pair of faces. If you focus on the white portion of the figure you would see a vase, while focusing on the black portion of the figure would show a pair of faces. The gestalt psychologists greatly emphasized on the fact that the same figure may be seen in either of the two ways. This shows that we do not passively respond to visual stimuli that fall on our retina but we try to organize and make sense of what we see. Hence perception is often seen as a constructive process that is beyond the stimuli presented to us and is an attempt to construct a meaningful situation.

Perceptual Grouping

The gestalt laws of perceptual grouping hold that objects in a scene appear to group according to certain laws or principles. Some of the laws of grouping are listed below:

1. **Similarity**: Objects with similar properties or that appear similar are grouped together (e.g. shape, color)

2. **Proximity**: Objects that are close by are grouped together.

3. **Good Continuation**: Objects that define smooth lines or curves are seen as one group than seeing them as incomplete and disjointed. It is the tendency to perceive a pattern in the most basic, organized and straightforward manner possible. In the figure below one would view it as two wavy lines rather than two curves opposite to each other.

1. **Symmetry**: Objects that form symmetrical patterns are grouped together.

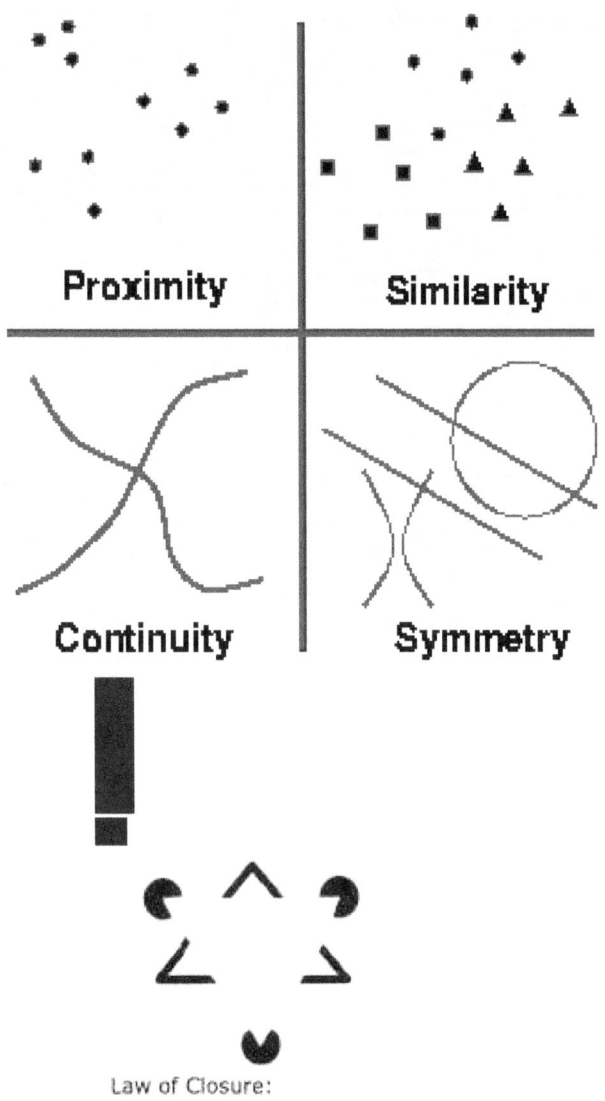

Law of Closure:

ERCEPTUAL GROUPING

Closure

        The Principle of Closure states that we tend to fill in missing bits, and perceive visuals as complete, or closed, entities. In other words it refers to the tendency to group according to enclosed or complete figures instead of open or incomplete ones.

In the above figure we see the black lines as forming a triangle instead of three small 'v' shaped brackets. Similarly, the black dots though incomplete are seen as dots than a broken figure. This explains the phenomenon of closure.

Another often quoted gestalt principle is that the whole is greater than its parts.

Perception of stimuli is beyond the individual elements that we sense. It represents an active, constructive process carried out by the brain by which bits and pieces of sensations are assembled together to make something greater and more meaningful than separate elements.

PERCEPTUAL CONSTANCIES

Objects are normally perceived to be constant in size, color and shape despite the fact that their retinal image change according to the conditions. The phenomenon by which

the physical objects are perceived as same in spite of changes in their physical appearance is called perceptual constancy.

When you stretch your right hand farther away from your body still you perceive it to be of the same size as that of your left hand. We do not see it as the right hand shrinking but realize that it is at a farther distance. This is due to size constancy. There are few types of perceptual constancies namely size constancy, color (or brightness) constancy and shape constancy.

Size Constancy

Though retinal image of object becomes smaller as the object moves to farther distance the viewer adjusts for this change as perceives the object to be of same size. A teenager standing at a farther distance from you is not seen as smaller in size than the teenager standing near you in front. Similarly, when you move away from a building you do not perceive the building shrinking but understand that it remains in the same size.

This phenomenon is called size constancy.

Color (or brightness) Constancy

Despite changes in illumination we see the object having same color. This is due to color constancy. When we see the same mug in different illumination we are still able to perceive all the sides of the mug as having the same color.

Shape Constancy

Though the retinal images of an object change when we view it from different angles we see the object to have same shape. Look at the pictures below for instance.

These are different pictures of the door, each in one position. When we see these pictures we do not perceive them as a change in shape, but perceive it to be of the same rectangular shape. This is possible due to shape constancy.

Perceptual constancy depends on our past experiences. This is obvious when we examine the behavior of people brought up in different cultures. An instance of this would be a study on Bambuti Pygmies. These pygmies live in dense forest in Zaire. Their vision is consistently limited to short distances. Due to this restriction they are deprived of the experiences that can help one to develop size constancy. They are found to have difficulty in judging the size of buffalo at a long distance that they mistook the buffalo to be some kind of an insect! This was reported by Colin Turnbull, an anthropologist, based on his first-hand experience with the pygmies.

Two theories attempt to explain the perceptual constancy phenomena.

Constructive theory holds that when we try to make inferences about the location of objects we greatly use our previous experience and expectations about the size of the object. Since we know the size of the particular object based on our earlier experience we easily make up for the changes in the size of the retinal image.

An alternative view proposed by James Gibson, referred to as ecological theory, suggests that relationship between objects in a scene gives us clue about the objects' size.

In addition to this information on the nature of the surfaces in the environment also helps us to judge the distance of the stimuli. Farther objects seem to have a different surface texture than those that are closer. Such differences provide us clue that help us to make judgments about depth.

Neither of the above theories independently explains all instances of perceptual constancies completely. Both construction and ecological processes work in combination.

DISTANCE PERCEPTION

Depth or location can be perceived even by a single sense organ. It is not always necessary to use both the eyes for perceiving depth. Certain cues, called the monocular cues, help us to perceive depth and distance even with just one eye.

Monocular Cues

Several strong monocular cues allow relative distance and depth to be judged. They are listed below:

1. Relative size
2. Interposition
3. Linear perspective
4. Aerial perspective
5. Height on plane
6. Texture gradient
7. Monocular movement parallax

Relative Size. Smaller objects are seen as farther from us. Hence the sizes of the objects tell us about the distance at which they are located. Objects furthest away are higher in our visual field. The closer an object is to the level of the horizon, the farther away an object appears.

Interposition. Interposition cues occur when there is overlapping of objects. The overlapped object is considered further away. Closer objects block out parts of objects that are farther. Hence complete objects are nearer to us than the objects that appear to be blocked.

> In the figure the lines that make up the gift boxed in the
> distance are hidden by the lines of the objects nearer to you.

Linear Perspective. P arallel objects converge when stretched into distance. This is a monocular cue in which distant objects appear to be closer together than nearer objects.

When objects of known distance subtend a smaller and smaller angle, it is interpreted as being further away. Parallel lines converge with increasing distance such as roads, railway lines, electric wires, etc.

In the above figure the lines that subtend a larger angle are judged to be closer than those that subtend a smaller angle.

Aerial Perspective. Objects that are far away appear fuzzier than closer objects since distance increases smog, dust, and haze thereby reducing the clarity of object. It is caused by the scattering of light in the atmosphere by small particles or vapor. Blue light, which has a shorter wavelength than other colors, is scattered more than the other colors. This scattering causes distant objects to appear slightly hazy and bluish in color. This also explains why mountains appear much closer on clear, dry days.

Height on plane. Objects that are higher on plane of view are seen as farther. n the above picture the tree on top half of the picture is seen as farther away than the tree that appears on the bottom half of the picture.

Texture gradient. The closer something is to us, the more detail and texture can we se.
As the distance increases the amount of texture lessens until it looks uniform. Elements closer are seen as father apart or less dense than objects farther away.

Motion parallax/ Relative Motion. The changes in position of the image of an object on the retina as our head moves provide a monocular cue for distance. Closer objects move greater distance rapidly than farther objects. When our heads move from side to side, objects at different distances move at a different relative velocity. Closer objects move
"against" the direction of head movement and farther objects move "with" the direction of head movement.

In addition to these one more of the cues comes from bending if the lens to focus on the nearby objects. This is referred to as accommodation. The sensations from the muscles attached to each eye lens flow to the brain. The changes in these sensations help

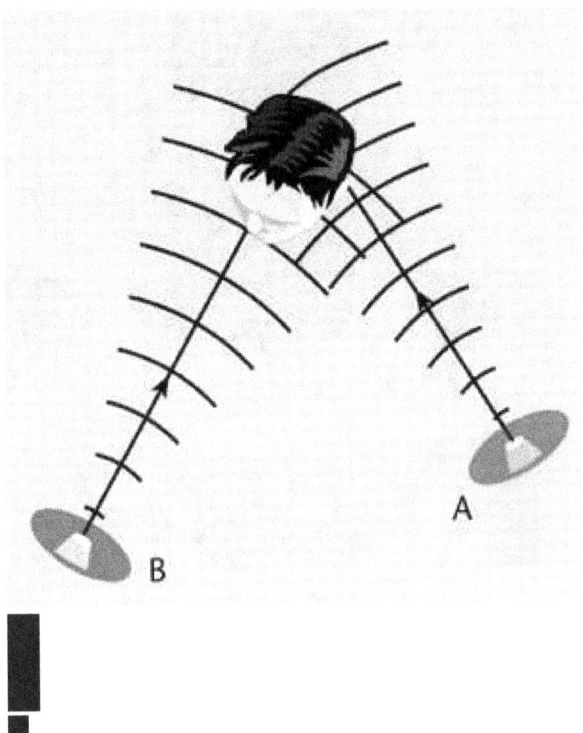

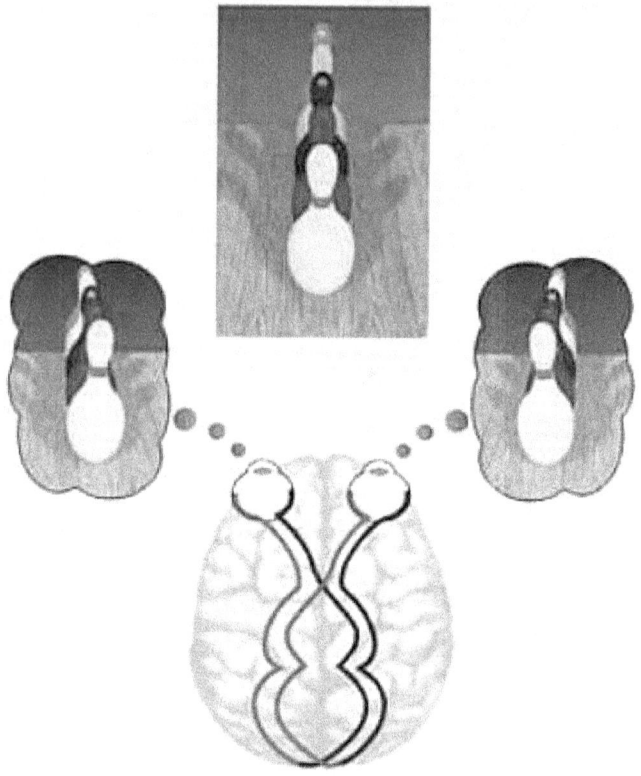

us to judge distances. Since this information is available even if we use only one eye it is a monocular cue.

Binocular Cues

When we see a distant object the lines of vision from our eyes are parallel.

However, eyes must converge to view closer objects, something that is at 50 feet or lesser in distance. This creates more muscle tension. The amount of strain or tension in the eye muscles while focusing on an object gives us a clue, referred to as **convergence**, to the depth at which the object is present. The muscles provide information to the brain regarding eye position in order to judge the distance. This may be seen in Picture a below.

Both our eyes are about 2.5 inches apart from each other. Due to the lateral displacement of our eyes, slightly dissimilar retinal images result from the perception of the same object from each eye. This results in **retinal disparity**. It is also referred to as binocular disparity. Stereoscopic vision occurs when both the retinal images are fused into one overall image that helps in perception of depth. Stereopsis is shown in Picture b below.

DEPTH PERCEPTION

Depth perception refers to the ability to see three-dimensional space and to judge distances accurately. Driving a car, riding a bike, shooting baskets, threading a needle or even walking around in the room would be almost impossible without this ability to perceive depth.

Depth perception is an important advantage for humans and other binocular animals. Both monocular and binocular cues are used to perceive depth. Not only does it give us an accurate sense of where objects are in relation to one another but also where we stand in relation to those same objects.

Visual Cliff Experiment

Some psychologists hold that depth perception is inborn while others argue that it is learned. It is likely that depth perception is partially innate and partially learned. The famous "Visual Cliff" experiments of the 1960's by Eleanor Gibson and Richard Walk is a classic experiment done to study development of depth perception which supports the hypothesis that depth perception could be partially innate and partially learned.

Visual cliff is a glass-topped table as shown in the picture above. A checkered surface lies directly beneath the glass surface on one side. On the other side the checkered surface lies about 4 feet below the glass surface of the table. Because of the above arrangement the glass looks like tabletop on one side of the table while it looks like a cliff, or drop-off, on the other side. The glass provided on the deeper side of the table prevents the babies from falling down.

The experiment involved babies as old as 6- to 14-months-old who were placed in the middle of the visual cliff. This provided them a choice of either coming to the shallow side or the deep side of the table. Most of the babies preferred to move to the shallow sides. Surprisingly, some babies refused to move to the deeper side even when their mothers tried calling them towards it.

The fact that babies as old as just six months old would not venture over a drop covered by glass (Gibson & Walk, 1960) implying that they are able to perceive depth at that age. This serves as evidence to the fact that depth perception in humans is either innate ability or learnt very early in life.

More recent studies have shown more interesting findings. Babies over nine months old when placed on the glass-covered drop have an increased heart rate, which could be perhaps showing that they are frightened. Babies less than six months of age actually showed a decrease in heart rate. Some other experiments have shown that the sight of their smiling mother on the other side of the drop will encourage the toddlers move across it, overriding their fear (Talaris, 2002).

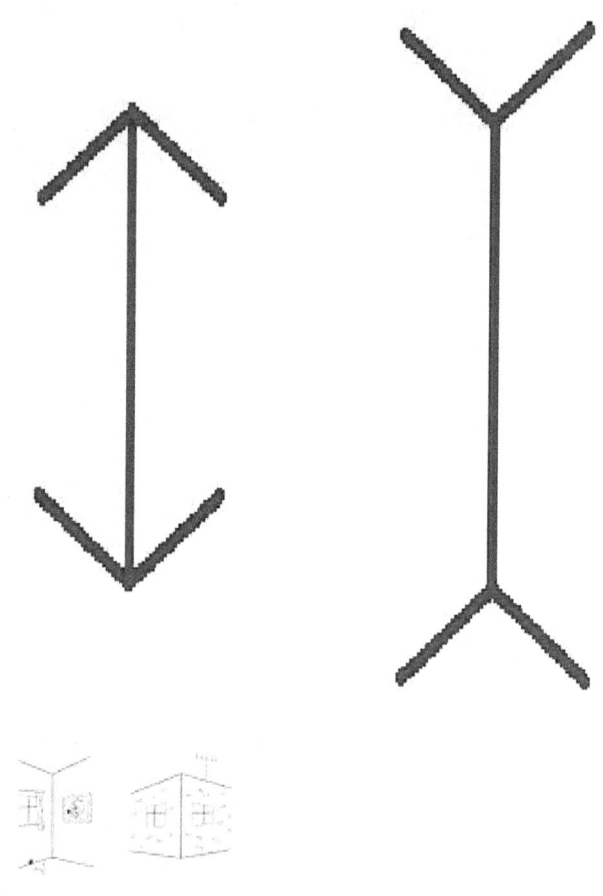

ILLUSION

Our perception gets largely altered with our experience. Perceptual learning refers to changes in perception that can be attributed to prior experience. These are caused due to changes in the brain that alter the way we process sensory information.

Illusions are false perceptions in which length, position, motion, curvature, or direction is consistently misjudged. Illusions are distorted perceptions of the stimuli that exist in reality unlike in hallucination the perception takes place in the absence of the actual sensory stimulus.

Perceptual learning results in a number of illusions. Size and shape constancy, habitual eye movement, continuity, and perceptual habits combine in various ways to produce a number of illusions. Some of the common illusions are Muller- Lyer Illusion, Poggendorff illusion, The Hermann grid, Ponzo illusion, and Moon Illusion to name a few.

In Muller- Lyer Illusion, as may be seen below, though the length of the two lines are the same we find the line enclosed by the feather-head is longer than the one enclosed by arrow- head (see picture a given below). This may be explained based on the real life experience with the edges and corners of rooms and buildings. The line with the featherhead is viewed as if it were the corner of the room viewed from inside (Gregory, 2000). In contrast, the line with the arrowhead is viewed as if it were the corner of a room seen from outside (see picture b given below). In short, our perception of two-dimensional designs is largely misguided by the cues that suggest a 3-D space.

If two objects make images of the same size then the more distant object must be definitely larger. This also explains Muller-Lyer Illusion. If the feather-headed line looks farther than the arrow-headed line then it has to be longer than the latter.

The above explanation, of course, presumes that the viewer has years of experience with straight lines and sharp edges. Groups of people in South Africa, the

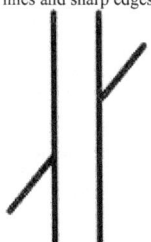

Zulus, live in a 'round' culture and they rarely encounter straight lines in their everyday life. They live in huts that are shaped like rounded mounds, their toys are round in shape and are curved, and there are no straight roads or rectangular buildings in their environment. Research on the Zulus report interesting findings. The Zulus hardly experience the Muller-Lyer illusion that confirms that past experiences and perceptual habits determine how we view the world.

We tend to perceive movement or motion when the objects rapidly change their positions. This is called as stroboscopic movement. This is typically seen in the strobe lights flashed on dance floors. Each time the strobe flashes it shows the dancers in a particular static position. But when the light flashes rapidly then normal motion is seen

Another well-known visual illusion is the Poggendorff Illusion (shown below). In the figure above it appears that the angular line that is on the left side of the parallel lines is at a higher plane as compared to the angular line that is on the right side of the parallel lines. However, one would find on extending the angular lines towards each other they are placed in exactly the same plane.

EXTRA SENSORY PERCEPTION

Though almost half of the general public believes in existence of extra-sensory perception (ESP) very few psychologists share this belief. It is seen that movies and television programs picture a lot of ESP and other paranormal phenomena as accepted facts. But how far are these facts are based on evidence is questionable.

ESP refers to the purported ability to perceive events in ways that cannot be explained by mere sensory capabilities. The study of ESP phenomena is the subject matter of the field of psychology called Parapsychology. Clairvoyance, telepathy, precognition and psychokinesis are few of the basic forms of ESP.

The purported ability that allows a person to perceive events or gain information in ways that appear to be unaffected by distance or normal/usual physical barriers is referred to as clairvoyance. Telepathy is one where one is able to have an extrasensory perception of another person's thoughts. To put it in simple terms, telepathy refers to the ability to read someone else's mind. The purported ability to perceive or to predict a future event is called precognition. This may take prophetic dreams that foretell future.

Under psychokinesis one is able top exert influence over inanimate object by will power.

Though this does not come under the realm of ESP it is often studied by parapsychologists.

If one has an apparent clairvoyant or telepathic experience he would be convinced that ESP exists. But to determine how much of the experience is beyond mere coincidence is always difficult.

Late.J.B.Rhine had done tremendous work in the area of psi events. Much of his experiments made use of the Zener cards that consists of a deck of 25 cards with each bearing one of five symbols. In a typical clairvoyant test the subjects were asked to guess the symbol of the cards as they were turned up from a shuffled deck of cards. A pure guess in this test generally produced an average score of 5 hits out of 25 cards.

None of the early experiments by Rhine using the Zener cards were valid for many reasons. The cards were poorly made that the symbols almost showed faintly on the back of the cards. Further there is also enough evidence that early experimenters had tendency to sometimes unconsciously give clues about the cards using their eyes.

Nevertheless, modern psychologists who are well aware of the need for double-blind experiments, security and accuracy in record keeping meticulous control. Hundreds of experiments have been reported in parapsychology journals that support psi abilities in the past one decade. Still psychologists are skeptical about psi abilities because fraud continues to plague this field. Especially in places where the purported psychic abilities are involved in making money more caution needs to be exerted in trusting the findings as valid.

Another major factor that stands as a drawback to research in parapsychology is inconsistency. Every study with positive findings has another study to prove it wrong.

ESP researches hold that this effect shows that parapsychology skills are very delicate.

On the other hand the critics argue that one scoring temporarily above change can only receive credit for run of luck. It is not fair to assume that the ESP is temporarily gone when the run is over. They emphasize on the point that all the runs must be counted and considered.

Many of the most spectacular studies in parapsychology cannot be replicated. The same researcher using the same experimental subjects cannot get the similar results every time. To add to this improved research methods usually result in fewer positive results.

This stands as a major drawback.

Another problem that plagues psi experiments in that of reinterpretation. For instance, ex-astronaut Edgar Mitchell worked on telepathetic experiments from space. In some trials, Mitchell claims, the 'receivers' scored above chance while the others scored

'below chance'. Though we might assume that below-chance trials were failures to find telepathy Mitchell interpreted them as 'successes'. He claimed that the 'failures' represented intentional 'psi missing'. Skeptics argue that if both high scores and low scores indicated success then what indicates failure!

Nevertheless, the outcome of many ESP studies is beyond debate. In a recent study that involved mass media, people attempted to identify ESP targets from a distance.

This enabled large scale testing of the ESP phenomena. The results of about 1.5 million ESP trials can be summarized in one single line: There was no significant ESP effect (Milton & Wiseman, 1999).

Results of various researches done on ESP phenomena for nearly 13 decades indicate that nothing conclusive can be said about the occurrence of psi events. Serious problems relating to evidence, procedure and scientific rigor are found in psi experiments. Survey of leading parapsychologists and skeptics by Blackmore (1989) reveal that belief in psi has decreased in contrast to the unconditional acceptance of psi by the media. Some researchers will, however, continue to attempt to prove the psi. Some would continue to remain skeptic considering the results of the huge body of research evidence available in the past 13 decades as good enough to abandon the concept of ESP

(Mark, 2000). One has to, at the least, exert caution in accepting the evidence reported by researchers who are uncritical 'believers'.

UNIT – IV INTELLINGENCE
Concepts and measurements of intelligence – theory of intelligence – mental health. Introduction to concept of mental health and classification of mental illness and retardation – mental deficiency.
THEORIES OF INTELLIGENCE
Numerous theories are available in literature that have made attempts to explain the construct intelligence. Some of them are focused on explaining the structure of intelligence. They have attempted to describe intelligence as made up of different components. On the other hand, some theories have tried to explain intelligence as a process. Some of the commonly referred theories are discussed below.
Factor Theory
Factor theories of intelligence focus on the structure of intelligence, that is, on the skills and abilities that it comprises of. In the course of development of intelligence theories several attempts have been made to slice the structure into different factors.

Factor analysis, a sophisticated procedure used to identify the constellation of variables in a domain has been used to identify the factors of intelligence. Factors refer to sources of differences seen among an array of variables.

Two Factor Theory. Charles Spearman (1940) put forth two- factor theory of intelligence to account for the variations seen in intelligence. This is the first widely influential theory of intelligence. Individuals who have the skill to quickly assemble colored blocks to match pictures of complex designs also found usually tending to perform well when they are given the task of assembling pieces of a puzzle. This as well as other behaviors that reflect an ability to visualize and manipulate patterns and forms in space suggests existence of a spatial ability factor. Spearman factor analyzed the scores of a large number of subjects on diverse tests that assessed many different intellectual skills and abilities. This enabled Spearman to assess which of these skills were related to each other. Based on the findings of the investigation the Spearman's model of intelligence was developed.

Spearman observed that some subject consistently scored high and a roughly equal number consistently scored low on all of the various tests purporting to assess different aspects of intelligence. People who scored high (or low) on one kind of test were found to obtain scores at a similar level on the other tests. But, their scores on various skill tests did tend to differ to some extent.

These observations influenced Spearman to propose that intelligence is made up of two components: a g- factor or general intelligence and a s-factor or special factor involving the collection of specific intellectual abilities. The existence of g-factor suggests that every individual has a certain level of general intelligence (g- factor), probably genetically determined, and it underlines all of our intelligent behavior. Every individual also has some specific abilities (s- factors) that are more useful in doing some tasks than in doing other tasks. General intelligence is needed for all, from plumber to philosopher to do their intellectual activity. Musical ability, mechanical ability, mathematical ability are special abilities and are emphasized by s- factor. S-Factor might vary from persona to person.

Spearman's 'g' factor theory of intelligence had been modified by Raymond Cattell (1905), his student. Cattle held that 'g' itself may considered to be a two part construct, gF and gC, which stand for *fluid and crystalized intelligence*. Fluid intelligence refers to ability to perceive relationships without previous specific experience as is measured with matrices tests or verbal analogies. Crystallized intelligence involves mental ability derived from previous experience as are measured by word meanings, use of tools and cultural practices. Crystalized intelligence may change over years in an individual due to decline in fluid knowledge.

Primary Mental Abilities. L.L.
Thustone, acritic of Spearman, defines intelligence as "Intelligence, considered as a mental trait, is the capacity to make impulses focal at their early, unfinished stage of formation. Intelligence is therefore the capacity for abstraction, which is an inhibitory process (Thurstone, 1924/1973)."

Thurstone rejects *g* was as statistical artifact resulting from the mathematical procedures used to study it. Adopting factor analysis, Thurstone found that intelligent behavior does not arise from a general factor, but rather emerges from seven independent factors. He named the factors identified by him the primary mental abilities. The *primary abilities*: word fluency, verbal comprehension, spatial visualization, number facility, associative memory, reasoning, and perceptual speed (Thurstone, 1938). Even in samples comprised of people with similar overall IQ scores, different profiles of primary mental abilities seem to result. Thus primary mental abilities seem to have clinical utility than Spearman's 'g'. However, in an intellectually heterogeneous group of children, he failed to find that the seven primary abilities were entirely separate, rather there existed an evidence for presence of 'g'. onsequently, Thurstone arrived at an elegant mathematical solution that resolved these apparently contradictory results. His final version of his theory of primary abilities was a compromise that accounted for the presence of both a general factor and the seven specific abilities.

The Seven Primary Mental Abilities (Thurston, 1938) are briefly described below:

Table 1. The Seven Primary Mental Abilities (Thurston, 1938)
Primary Mental Ability Factor
 Nature of the ability implied by the Factor
Verbal Comprehension understanding the meaning of words, concepts and ideas Numerical Ability using numbers in order to quickly compute answers to problems Spatial Relations visualizing and manipulating patterns and forms in space. Perceptual Speed grasping perceptual details quickly and accurately; determining similarities and differences between various stimuli. Word Fluency using words quickly and fluently while performing tasks like rhyming, solving anagrams, and doing crossword puzzles. Memory recalling information.Inductive Reasoning driving general rules and principles from the information that is presented.

Structure of Intellect.

J.P.Guilford has propounded a three-dimensional model of intelligence. His theory of intelligence is termed the Structure of Intellect (SI) theory. The theory views intelligence as comprising of operations, contents, and products.

Succinctly the model suggest that Five kinds of operations carried on five kinds of contents yield six kinds of products, and as such one hundred and fifty elements of

CONTENTS — VISUAL / AUDITORY / SYMBOLIC / SEMANTIC / BEHAVIORAL

PRODUCTS — UNITS / CLASSES / RELATIONS / SYSTEMS / TRANSFORMATION / IMPLICATIONS

OPERATIONS — EVALUATION / CONVERGENT PRODUCTION / DIVERGENT PRODUCTION / MEMORY / COGNITION

intellect could be generated and identified as constituting and accounting for the structure of intellect. The five kinds of intellectual operations include cognition, memory, divergent production, convergent production, evaluation; the six kinds of products include units, classes, relations, systems, transformations, and implications; and, the five kinds of contents include visual, auditory, symbolic, semantic, behavioral tasks. . Since each of these dimensions is independent, there are theoretically 150 different components of intelligence possible to be identified and tested.

Picture Courtesy: http://ehlt.flinders.edu.au/education/DLT/2002/dltwsite/guilf.htm
The Structure of Intellect (SI) Model of J.P.Guilford.

Guilford adopted factor analysis and developed a wide variety of psychometric tests to measure the specific abilities predicted by SI theory. The tests provide an operational definition of the many abilities proposed by the theory. The convergent and divergent production operations are recognized to be synonymous with intelligence and creativity.

Process Approaches

The factorial approaches of Spearman, Thurston, and Guilford have contributed to our understanding of the structure of intelligence as comprising of several factors. They imply that the concept that intelligence may comprise many separate abilities that operate more or less independently was established. However they do not address the important question of how people solve problems and interact effectively (i.e. intelligently) with their environments. In the last decades new theoretical models of intelligence that seek to understand intelligence as process have emerged in the field. The multiple intelligence model and the triarchic theory of intelligence theories of Howard Gardner and Robert Sternberg represent approaches different to the one adopted by earlier psychologists.

Multiple Intelligence. Based on the findings from fields as disparate as artificial intelligence, developmental psychology, and neurology, a number of investigators have put forth the view that the mind consists of several independent modules or

"intelligences." Howard Gardener has developed his *theory of multiple intelligences*, and argues that human beings have evolved to be able to carry out at least seven separate forms of analysis. The seven intelligences identified by Gardner include Linguistic intelligence (as in a poet); Logical- mathematical intelligence (as in a scientist); Musical intelligence (as in a composer); Spatial intelligence (as in a sculptor or airplane pilot); Bodily kinesthetic intelligence (as in an athlete or dancer); Interpersonal intelligence (as in a salesman or teacher); and Intrapersonal intelligence (exhibited by individuals with accurate views of themselves). Gardner suggests that "although they are not necessarily dependent on each other, these intelligences seldom operate in isolation. Every normal individual possesses varying degrees of each of these intelligences, but the ways in which intelligences combine and blend are as varied as the faces and the personalities of individuals."

Triarchic Theory of Intelligence. Sternberg (1979, 1981 and 1982) has proposed a theory of Practical intelligence. This theory has departed from adopting a psychometric approach to intelligence and creativity and leaned heavily on information processing approach in studying intelligence. The initial approach to developing this theory focused on how information is processed by people in order to solve problems and deal effectively with their environments. The steps people go through when solving the kinds of problems typically encountered in intelligence tests involve six steps. These steps include. *Encoding* comprising of identifying the key terms or concepts in the problems and retrieving any relevant information from Long Term Memory, Inferring referring to determining the nature of relationships that exist between these terms or concepts, *Mapping* referring to Clarifying the relationship between previous situations and the present one, *Application* involving deciding if the information about known relationships can be applied to the present problem, *Justification* involving deciding if the answer can be justified and *Response* referring to providing the best possible answer, based on proper information processing at each of the previous stages.

Sternberg believes that people can be taught to construct their own problem solving strategies by learning to think about how they approach problems and how to function more effectively. Thus by teaching more effectively, intelligence of the individual, at least as measured by intelligence tests, can be increased. Sternberg's (1985-86) has expanded his information – processing approach recently. He calls it the triarchic theory of intelligence. According to this theory, intelligence is defined as a multidimensional trait that is comprised of three different abilities: Componential, Experiential, and Contextual

Sternberg has developed his Triarchic Theory of Human Intelligence (1977, 1985, 1995). TheTriarchic Theory seems to be an attempt to synthesize the various theories of intelligence. Sternberg views Intelligence as,"Purposive adaptation to, shaping of, and selection of real-world environments relevant to one's life" (Sternberg, 1984, p.271).

Intelligence is purposive in that it is directed towards goals, however vague or subconscious it may be. Thus, intelligence is indicated by one's attempts to adapt to one's environment. He subsumes both Spearman's *g* and underlying information processing components to account for intelligence. His theory includes three facets or subtheories of intelligence including Analytical (componential) Intelligence, Creative (experiential) Intelligence, and Practical (contextual) Intelligence.

Sternberg's theory builds on his earlier componential approach to reasoning and is mostly based on observing Yale graduate students. He believes that intelligence properly defined and assessed will manifest in real- life success as he observed amongst his students.

Componential subtheory. Analytical Intelligence (Academic problem-solving skills) is based on the joint operations of metacomponents and performance components and knowledge acquisition components of intelligence, The metacomponents seem to control, monitor and evaluate cognitive processing. Such tasks are the *executive* functions to order and organize performance and knowledge acquisition components.

They involve the higher order mental processes that order and organize the performance components. They are used to analyze problems and pick a strategy for solving them.

They determine what to do and the performance components actually carryout them.

The performance components are the basic operations in any cognitive act. They execute strategies assembled by the metacomponents. The cognitive processes enable one to encode stimuli, hold information in short-term memory, make calculations, perform mental calculations, mentally compare different stimuli, retrieve information from long-term memory.

The knowledge acquisition components are the processes used in gaining and storing new knowledge. They are concerned with capacity for learning. Strategies used to help memorize things provide an instance of the processes involved in this category.

Individual differences in intelligence are hence related to individual differences witnessed in the use of these cognitive processes. Individuals with better reasoning ability generally spend more time understanding the problem but reach their solution faster than those who are less skilled at the task

Experiential Subtheory. Creative Intelligence involves insights, synthesis and the ability to react to novel situations and stimuli. Creative intelligence is the experiential aspect of intelligence. It reflects how an individual connects the internal world to external reality.

The Creative facet consists of the ability that allows people to think creatively and that which allows people to adjust creatively and effectively to new situations.

More intelligent individuals will also move from consciously learning in a novel situation to automating the new learning so that they can attend to other tasks.

It is assumed that the novelty skills and automatization skills are the two broad classes of abilities associated with intelligence. A task measures intelligence if it requires the ability to deal with novel demands or the ability to automatize information processing, two ends of a continuum. Hence, novel tasks or situations are good measures of intellectual ability. They assess an individual's ability to apply existing knowledge to new problems.

Contextual Subtheory. Practical Intelligence involves the ability to grasp, understand and deal with everyday tasks. This is the Contextual aspect of intelligence and reflects Analytical Facet. Analytical Intelligence is similar to the standard psychometric definition of intelligence. Measured by Academic problem solving: analogies and puzzles belong to this category. This corresponds to Sternberg's earlier componential intelligence. This reflects how an individual relates to his internal world.

Practical Intelligence may be said to be intelligence that operates in the real world. Individuals with this type of intelligence can adapt to, or shape their environment.

It might also be called 'Street-smarts'. In measuring this facet, not only mental skills but also attitudes and emotional factors that influence intelligence are to be included. The practical intelligence is a combination of adaptation to the environment in order to have goals met, changing the environment in order to have goals met and if the two preceding acts are not working, moving to a new environment in which goals can be met.

Individuals considered intelligent in one culture may be looked on as unintelligent in another. Sternberg's theory is distinguished from other theories by not defining

intelligence in terms of psychometric intelligence tests rather than performance in the everyday world.

ASSESSMENT OF INTELLIGENCE

Alfred Binet, the French psychologist published the first modern version of intelligence test called the Binet-Simon intelligence scale, in 1905. He originally evolved the test to identify students who needed special help in coping with the school curriculum. Binet published revisions of his intelligence scale in 1908 and 1911. A further refinement of the Binet-Simon scale was published in in 1916 by Lewis Terman, the American Psychologist. Terman incorporated the suggestion of William Stern, the German psychologist that an individual's intelligence level be measured as an (I.Q.).

Terman named the as the Standford-Binet. This scale formed the basis for one of the modern intelligence tests still commonly used today.

The Classical Tests of Intelligence

The introduction of the Stanford-Binet IQ test initiated the modern intelligence test movement. The test employed questions of increasing difficulty, and included such items as attention, memory, and verbal skills. Terman had removed several of the Binet-Simon test items and added completely new ones. The test gained acceptability and Rober Yerkes , the President of the American Psychological Association decided to use the test to develop the *Army Alpha* and *Army Beta* tests, which helped classify recruits to the Army. Thus, a high- scoring individual would get a grade of A (high officer material), whereas a low-scoring individual would get a grade of E and be rejected (Fancher, 1985).

The Stanford-Binet test under went several revisions and by the time the fifth edition of the test came up it had been adminsitered to more a stratified sample of 4800 subjects and norms have been developed on the data obtained on the sampele. By then the test had been found to have adequate validity as shown by correlation with the previous versions as well as other tests including WAIS.- III R. The Binet-Simon Fifth Edition included Fluid Reasoning , Knowledge, Quantitative Reasoning, Visual-Spatial Processing, and Working Memory as the five factors tested. Each of these factors is tested in two separate domains, verbal and nonverbal. Test items like verbal analogies used to test Verbal Fluid Reasoning and picture absurdities used to test Nonverbal Knowledge provide illustrtion of the type of items included in the test.It was suggeste that students with exceptional scores on this test may be deemed bright, moderately gifted, highly gifted, extremely gifted, or profoundly gifted in contrast to thethose who score poorly on this test.

Applying the propertie of normal curve deviation of the subjects from the average was traced and used for identifying gifted as well as the individuals who had lower levels of intelligence were identified. The various rvisions of Standford-Binet Scales are presented in table below.

Wechsler Adult Intelligence Scale o r **WAIS** is a general test of intelligence (IQ). The test was first published in 1955 as a revision of the Wechler-Bellevue Test (1939). The later was a battery of tests that is composed from subtests Wechsler

"adopted" from the Army Tests (Yerkes, 1921). Weschler defined intelligence as the global capacity of a person to act purposefully, to think rationally, and to deal effectively with his/her environment.

WAIS comprises of 14 sub tests. There are 7 verbal sub tests and 7 nonverbal or performance sub tests in WAIS. Wechsler's tests provide three scores including a verbal IQ (VIQ) , a performance IQ (PIQ) and a composite, single **full-scale** IQ score based on the combined scores. The WAIS-R was standardized on a sample of 1,880 subjects in the age group ranging from 16 to 74. The current version is WAIS-III (1997). The median score of the sample on the full-scale IQ is centered at 100 with a standard deviation of 15.

The WAIS-III is appropriate for assessing intelligence throughout adulthood and for use with those individuals over 74 years of age. WAIS, 7 – 16 yrs is used for assessing the IQ of the children aged between 7 to 16. Wechsler Preschool and Primary Scale of Intelligence (WPPSI, 2 ½ - 7 yrs) For persons under 16, the Wechsler Intelligence Scale for Children (WISC,

7-16 yrs) and the Wechsler Preschool and Primary Scale of Intelligence (WPPSI, 2 1/2-7 yrs) is used.to assess IQ of the chilred in the age group of 2 ½ to 7 years. WAIS provides an IQ score in case only performance tests were adminsitered.

A short, four-subtest, version of the battery has recently beenmade available. This permits clinicians to form a validated estimate of verbal, performance and full scale IQ in a shorter amount of time. The Wechsler Abbreviated Scale of Intelligence (WASI) uses the vocabulary, similarities, block design and matrix reasoning subtests of the WAIS to provide an estimate of the full IQ scores.

The 14 subtests of the WAIS-III

C.Raven (1938) developed the Progressive Matrices. They popularly used tests of reasoning and clear thinking. They are well known as non verbal tests of abstract reasoning. Each item presents a matrix with a specific pattern and the respondent is asked to identify the missing segment required to complete a larger pattern. The test items are presented in the form of a 3x3 or 2x2 matrix, giving the test its name.

The matrices are available in three different forms for testing the participants of different ability:

Standard Progressive Matrices were the original form of the matrices, published in 1938. The booklet comprises five sets (A to E) of 12 items each. The items within a set become increasingly difficult, requiring ever greater cognitive capacity to encode and analyze information. The items are presented in black ink on a white background.

Coloured Progressive Matrices was designed for use with younger children, the elderly, and people with moderate or severe learning difficulty. This test contains sets A and B from the standard matrices, with a further set of 12 items inserted between the two, as set Ab. Mostof the items are presented on a coloured background to make the test visually stimulating for the test taker. The very last few items in set B are presented as black-on-white. By this way, if participants performance surpassed the tester's expectations, transition to sets C, D, and E of the standard matrices is fecilitated.

Advanced Progressive Matrices contains 48 items, presented as one set of 12 (set I), and another of 36 (set II). Items are presented in black ink on a white background, and become increasingly difficult as progress is made through each set. The items are appropriate for adults and adolescents of above average intelligence.

The parallel forms of the standard and coloured progressive matrices were published in 1998. An extended form of the standard progressive matrices, *Standard Progressive Matrices Plus*, was also published at the same time, offering greater discrimination among more able young adults.Raven's Progressive Matrices and Vocabulary tests measure the two main components of general intelligence (Spearman's g): the ability to think clearly and make sense of complexity, known as eductive ability and the ability to store and reproduce information, known as reproductive ability.

Culture-fair Intelligence Test

Culture- fair intelligence tests are also called culture- free tests. They are designed to assess intelligence without relying on knowledge specific to any individual cultural group. The first culture- fair test developed to assess intelligence was the Army Examination Beta which was developed by the United States military during World War II to screen recruits of average intelligence who were illiterate or for whom English was a second language. From the postwar period, culture-fair tests, which rely largely on nonverbal questions were used in public schools with Hispanic students and other non-native-English speakers who were not having familiarity with both English language and American culture.

Cattell's Culture Fair Intelligence Test (CFIT). Raymond Cattell developed *the Culture Fair Intelligence Test. (CFIT).* The Cattell Culture Fair Series consist of scales one to three for ages four and four onward. The scales are intended to assess intelligence independent of cultural experience, verbal ability, or educational level.

The tests consist mostly of paper-and-pencil questions involving the relationships between figures and shapes. Parts of scale one, used with the youngest age group, utilize various objects instead of paper and pencil. Activities in scales two and three, for children age eight and eight onwards, include completing series, classifying, and filling in incomplete designs

Sternberg Multidimensional Abilities Test (STAT). Sternberg published

Sternberg Multidimensional Abilities Test (STAT) in 1992. The STAT is a battery of multiple-choice questions. The battery divided into nine multiple levels for differing ages, and will be suitable for group administration to individuals in kindergarten through college, as well as to adults. Two forms of the test are be available The questions purport to tap into the three independent aspects of intelligence including analytic, practical and creative ones proposed in Sternberg's triarchic theory of intelligence. The STAT

measures three abilities including analytical, creative and practical using both multiple choice and essay questions. It yields separate scores for componential information processing (analytical ability), coping with novelty (synthetic ability) and (as a separate score) automatization and practical- intellectual skills. Crossed with these scores are scores for three content areas including verbal, quantitative, and figural. The various kinds of processing are each measured in each of the three content domains, yielding 4 x 3 = 12 separate subtests per level. It is possible to diagnose not only strengths and weaknesses in information processing, but also in various kinds of representations of information. The test is a group test, and can be administered in its totality in three class periods. Portions of can also be administered in the class in lesser period. Thus, the scores provided by the test correspond strictly to the aspects of intelligence specified by the Triarchic Theory. The theory specified that intelligence can be understood in terms of components of information processing being applied to relatively novel experience and later being automatized in order to serve three functions in the environment: adaptation to, selection of, and shaping of that environment. All the measures are considered important to success in life and have been used to develop programs for children and to select business managers. Together, the three measures provided more information than just the analytical intelligence measured by standard IQ tests.

The STAT test items differ from those on conventional tests of intelligence. There is more emphasis on ability to learn than on what has been learned. For instance, verbal skill is measured by learning from context, not by vocabulary (which represents products rather than processes of learning). The test measures skills for coping with novelty, whereby the examinee must imagine a hypothetical state of the world (such as cats being magnetic) and then reason as though this state of the world were true. The test measures practical abilities, such as reasoning about advertisements and political slogans, not just about decontextualized words or geometric forms. These are only a few of the differences that separate this test from its predecessors claimed by its author. Sternberg admits that the STAT is not immune to effects of prior learning, nor is it "culture- free." However, he states that his test seems broader and more comprehensive than other existing tests, and hence allows for more diversity in backgrounds than would be true of typical tests.

Mental retardation

Mental retardation is regarded as a developmental disability. It first appears in children under the age of 18. Mental disorder is defined as an intellectual functioning level that is well below average and significant limitations in daily living skills. The level of intellectual functioning is determined by using standard intelligence tests and considering the IQ obtained on them. The living skills connote the adaptive functioning.

Description. Mental retardation begins in childhood or adolescence, before the age of 18, and persists throughout adulthood in most cases. An individual diagnosed as having mental retardation if he or she has an intellectual functioning level well below average and significant limitations in two or more adaptive skill areas. Mental retardation is operationally defined as IQ score below 70-75 on standardized tests that measure the ability to reason. Adaptive skills include the ability to produce and understand language (communication), home- living skills, use of community resources, health, safety, leisure, self-care, and social skills, self-direction, functional academic skills (reading, writing, and arithmetic), and work skills.

Mentally retarded children reach developmental milestones such as walking and talking much later than the general population. Symptoms of mental retardation may appear at birth or later in childhood, and the time of onset depends on the suspected cause of the disability. In certain cases of mild mental retardation, diagnosis may not be made before the child enters preschool. Because, in these cases, the children typically have difficulties with social, communication, and functional academic skills which could be observed prior to they entering the school. Children with a neurological disorder or illness such as encephalitis or meningitis may suddenly show signs of cognitive impairment and adaptive difficulties.

Mental retardation varies in severity. *The Diagnostic and Statistical Manual of Mental Disorders,* Fourth Edition (*DSM-IV*) is the diagnostic standard for professionals in mental health in the United States. The *DSM-IV* classifies four different degrees of mental retardation: *mild, moderate, severe*, and *profound.* These categories are based on the functioning level of the individual.

Mild mental retardation. Children who have their IQ score range from 50-75, are diagnosed for mild mental retardation. They can often acquire academic skills up to the 6th grade level. The mildly retarded can become fairly self-sufficient and in some cases, live independently, with community and social support.

Moderate mental retardation. Children who have their IQ score range from 35-55, are diagnosed for moderate mental retardation. Moderately retarded individuals can carry out work and self-care tasks with moderate supervision. They typically acquire communication skills in childhood and are able to live and function successfully within the community in a supervised environment.

Severe mental retardation. Children who have their IQ score range from 20-40, are diagnosed for severe mental retardation. Severely retarded individuals may master very basic self-care skills and some communication skills. Many severely retarded individuals are able to live in a group home.

Profound mental retardation. Children who have their IQ score range from 20-25, are diagnosed for profound mental retardation. Profoundly retarded individuals may be able to develop basic self-care and communication skills with appropriate support and training. Their retardation is often caused by an accompanying neurological disorder, and they need a high level of structure and supervision.

The American Association on Mental Retardation (AAMR) has also developed another widely accepted diagnostic classification system for mental retardation focusing on the capabilities of the retarded individual rather than on the limitations. The categories used in this classification system describe the level of support required. They are: *intermittent support, limited support, extensive support*, a n d *pervasive support*. The AAMR classification mirrors the *DSM-IV* classification. Intermittent support, for instance, refers to support needed only occasionally, during times of stress or crisis. This the type of support typically required for most mildly retarded individuals. Pervasive support, or life-long, daily support for most adaptive areas, would be required for the profoundly retarded.

UNIT – V PERSONALITY
Meaning – determinants of personalities – defense mechanism – theory of personality – measurement of personality. Adjustment – concept of adjustment and maladjustments – stress – frustration and conflict sources of frustration conflicts – nature and types of conflicts.
Dynamics of Personality
An individual's life is dominated by conflict between Id, ego, and super ego.

Individual's mind is a field for constant battles between the id, ego, and superego. The id always insists instant gratification of its felt needs. The ego has to rise to the occasion and control the Id impulses. The super ego must invoke the guilt feeling to obtain the Id impulses completely. Usually these conflicts are centered on sex and aggression. This is because that the social norms governing the sexual behavior and aggression are so subtle. It is also the case that most often inconsistent messages about what's appropriate to deal with sexual and aggressive impulses are passed on to the individual by the society. Hence these drives create a lot of confusion. Hence, ordinarily these drives are thwarted more than other basic biological needs.

Anxiety and Defense Mechanisms. Most of the conflicts confronting an individual are usually trivial and are subjected to get resolved within a short span. Yet, a few conflicts can persist for a long time. Such conflicts are the conflicts the individual experiencing the conflict might not be aware of since they are rooted in his unconscious.

These conflicts can produce anxiety that that slips to the surface of conscious awareness.

The anxiety so experienced may be attributed to the concerns of the ego. The ego in such a condition may be worried about the Id getting out of control and leading to severe negative consequences. The ego may also be concerned that the super ego is getting out of control leading to feelings of guilt about real or thwarted transgression of the moral doctrines. The anxiety arising in these conditions is quite distressing to the individual experiencing the conflict. Under such conditions, individuals may resort to a variety of strategies to get over the unpleasant experience of anxiety. The strategies so attempted may constitute largely unconscious reactions that ward of the anxiety and guilt feelings to certain extant during a span of time. Since they are self-deceptive they do not provide ultimate solution to the problems of haunting anxiety and tormenting guilt feelings. Such strategies are termed defense mechanisms in psychoanalysis.

Mental Mechanisms. Several are the strategies of the ego to ward of anxiety and guilt feelings. *Repression* is an active defense mechanism by which the ego attempts to push away the anxiety arousing impulses or memories into the unconscious. Keeping distressing thoughts and feelings buried in the unconscious constitutes this process. This could be explained by the instance of a woman who was sexually abused in childhood develops amnesia for the event. In *denial,* an individual may just refuse to acknowledge anxiety-arousing conditions of the environment. Such denial may involve either the emotions attendant with the event or the event itself. Denial connotes the motivated negation. Here, ego tries to evade the disagreeable realities by refusing to acknowledge them and arguing against them. Most people who are diagnosed for having diabetic disorder for the first time usually attempt to ward of their anxiety by denying that they have the disorder. They often feel that the diagnosis is erroneous. In *displacement* or *scapegoating* and unacceptable dangerous impulse is repressed and there upon shifted to another substitute target with which the individual could show his reaction in a safe manner. A person tormented by the boss at his office might not show any revolt at the office since he cannot do so. But, he may turn to his helpless wife and children and show his reactions I the form of aggression. In *projection* an individual might resort to attribute the forbidden impulses to others. A stingy person might project his unacceptable character of stinginess to others and call every other person a stingy one. Constructing false but plausible excuses to an unacceptable anxiety provoking experience or event might constitute *rationalization*. In rationalization one resort to argue a case, which is not acceptable to him at the unconscious, level and builds up an apparent rational excuse. A research scholar failing in an exam may argue that the teachers had not valued his paper in a proper manner and the teacher who valued his script had taken revenge on him since he might have been jealousy of the brilliancy of the scholar. In this mechanism an individual might also invoke *sour grapism* arguing that what he could not achieve is not worth achieving. In *reaction formation* an individual might resort to an exaggerated expression of the behavior that stands exactly opposite to what he desires to adopt in his unconscious mind. The police officer who recklessly beat a culprit of a petty offense might be entertaining criminal cravings in his unconscious and the criminal craving impulses repressed might be contributing to his resorting to this mechanism. Some time an individual who could not successfully cope with present challenge might fell anxious and guilty and repress the feelings. Such repressed feeling may be expressed by his reverting to an earlier stage of his development. This state of affairs is called *regression*.

A research scholar who cries hysterically when he is told that he had not passed in a paper might be in this state. In *identification* an individual might identify himself with some other person who may be a hero or an aggressor to ward of his repressed anxiety. Bolstering self-esteem by forming an imaginary or real alliance with a person or a group might explain the mechanism of identification. In *sublimation* an individual may accept a goal alternative to the goal he could not achieve, and which provides a socially acceptable outlet of expression and yields partial satisfactions that are free of guilt feelings. Sublimation is regarded the healthiest of all the defense mechanisms used by individuals. An individual given to aggressive impulses turning himself to boxing and the an individual with sex-curiosity diverting his curiosity by becoming a scientist are examples for sublimation. *Compensation* is another healthy mechanism in which the individual attempts to disguise the presence of a weak or undesirable trait by emphasizing a desirable one. A person with stuttering might turn all his efforts to develop excellence in writing scripts may take up the writing talent to compensate his deficiency in speaking.

However, it should be quickly added that over compensation might prove unhealthy in its outcome. An unattractive girl trying to compensate her felt deficiency by trying to become a very interesting speaker must be well with in her limits. Lest she might be called chatterbox and might have to be anxious about people rejecting her in the area in which she attempts compensation. In *fantasy* or *daydreaming* an individual tries to invoke imagination and imagine that he achieves his goals and desires. It stands for a subjective reverie that provides some comfort when the individual is far away from his desired goal in reality. Building castles in air is another term used to denote this mechanism. Some time indulging in this mechanism might induce such strong involvement that the individual might resort to action in overt behavior. A young adolescent vendor selling glasswares was day dreaming that he will be able to build up his business and become a great rich man one day. While he had been engrossed in such fantasy he assumed that he had already become and imagined that he might kick his subordinate with his foot. He felt that this fantasy was so real that he indeed kicked with his foot in front and the glass wears in front of him were damaged by his kicking.

Authoritarianism and Dogmatism:

People who are likely to have authoritarian orientation tend to use their power more aggressively towards their subordinates and create a very defensive climate in the department, while at the same time they are being very submissive or docile towards their supervisors. Dogmatism refers to the extent to which people are flexible or rigid in dealing others. Managers who are exhibiting these traits are likely to be detached from others and people show much of hatredness in them.

A combination of high authoritarianism and dogmatism is obviously not conducive to creativity and organizational effectiveness since new ideas that people at lower levels in the system have will neither be listened to nor implemented. Certain societies tend to accept authority much better than others, and hence authoritarianism can be traced to needs of dependency in members in some cultures who feel comfortable when they are 'told' the ways in which things have to be carried out in their work.

Machiavellianism:

This refers to the extent to which people are manipulative and tactic in achieving one's own goals. These people strongly believe that ends can justify means. People who are high Machiavellian tend to be cool, willing to twist and turn facts to influence others and try to gain control of people, events, and situations by manipulating the system to their advantage. High Machiavellians may be successful only for a short period but in long run they tend to be distrusted and disliked by many in the department and finally they may be ineffective.

High-Machiavellians manipulates more, win more, are persuaded less and have a grater influence over other people than do low-Machiavellians. Yet these High-Machiavellians outcomes are moderated by situational factors. It has been found that High-Machiavellians flourish:

· when they interact face-to-face with others rather than indirectly

· when the situation has a minimum number of rules and regulations, thus allowing latitude for improvisation

· where emotional involvement with details irrelevant to winning distracts low-Machiavellianism

· when forming coalitions which they use to their advantage.

The following are the strategies to protect against the manipulative actions of High-Machiavellians:

i) Expose them to others: Expose the broken promises, manipulative strategies and lies of high-Machiavellian to others.

ii) Pay attention to what people do, not to what they say: High-Machiavellians make great promises and are great persuaders, so pay attention to the action that a person carries out and avoid being swayed by smooth promises

iii) Avoid situations that give high-Machiavellians the edge: Do not make decisions quickly where emotions are high and a person puts forward a persuasive argument and pushes for an immediate decision. Try not to face this person on a one-to-one basis. Invites others to participate in the meeting. : **Risk Taking**

This refers to the extent to which people are willing to take chances. This propensity to assume or to avoid risk has been shown to have an effect on their decision making capabilities and information gathering process. High risk taking managers made more rapid decision and used less information in making their choices than did the low risk taking managers.

The requirement of Risk taking propensity varies from the different types of job demands.

For instance, a high risk taking propensity may lead to more effective performance for a stockbroker in brokerage firm than an accountant whose job demands more cautious approach in dealing each and every one of the things. An accountant performing auditing activities is expected to have low-risk taking propensity as his nature of job demands to follow a book of rules and regulations.

Type A and Type B Personality:

This refers to the extent to which people tend exhibit certain characteristics. Type A person feels a chronic sense of time urgency, are highly achievement oriented, exhibit a competitive drive and are impatient when their work is slowed down for any reason.

Type B persons are easygoing individuals who do not have sense of time urgency, and who do not experience the competitive drive.

Type A Mangers do operate under moderate to high level of stress. They subject themselves to more or less continuous time pressure, creating for themselves a life of deadlines. These characteristics result in some rather specific behavior outcomes. For example, Type A people are fast workers because they emphasize quantity over quality.

In managerial positions, Type A executives demonstrate their competitiveness by working long hours and not infrequently making poor decisions because they make them too quickly. Type A's are also rarely creative. Because of their concern with quantity and speed, they rely on past experiences when faced with problems. They do not allocate the time that is necessary to develop unique solutions to new problems.

Which category of people – Type A or Type B more successful in organization? The research results reported that great sales people are usually Tape A category. But the senior executives are likely to be Type B category. The main reason is that Type A people are usually trade off quality of effort for quantity. Promotions in corporate and professional organization usually go to those who are wise rather than to those who are merely hasty, to those who are tactful rather than to those who are hostile, and to those who are creative rather than to those who are merely agile in competitive strife.

The following are their typical characteristics of Type A and Type B people. Type A people are likely to more chances to get coronary heart diseases than Type B people.

Type A Personality
· Competitive
· High Need for Achievement
· Aggressive
· Works Fast
· Impatient
· Restless
· Extremely Alert
· Tense Facial Muscles
· Constant Time Pressure

Type B Personality
· Able to Take Time to Enjoy Leisure
· Not Preoccupied with Achievement
· Easy Going Works at Steady Pace
· Seldom Impatient
· Relaxed
· Not Easily Frustrated
· Moves Slowly
· Seldom Lacks Enough Time

Tolerance for Ambiguity

This dimension refers to the extent to which individuals are threatened by or have difficulty coping with situations that are ambiguous, where change occurs rapidly or predictably, where information is inadequate or unclear or where complexity exists. This personality characteristic indicates the level of uncertainty that people can tolerate with out experiencing undue stress and can still function effectively. Managers with higher tolerance of ambiguity scores are more likely to be entrepreneurial in their actions, to screen out less information in a complex environment, and to choose specialties in their occupations those possess less-structured tasks. It is also reported that individuals who are more tolerant of ambiguity have more difficulty focusing on a single important element of information – they are inclined to pay attention to a variety of items – and they may have somewhat less ability to concentrate without being distracted by interruptions.

There are three dimensions in Tolerance of Ambiguity. They are Novelty, Complexity and Insolubility.

Tolerance of Ambiguity towards Novelty: This refers to the extent to which you are tolerant of new, unfamiliar information or situations.

Tolerance of Ambiguity towards Complexity: This refers to the extent to which you are tolerant of multiple, distinctive or unrelated information.

Tolerance of Ambiguity towards Insolubility: This refers to the extent to which you are tolerant of problems that are very difficult to solve alternative solutions are not evident, information is unavailable or the problems compensate seem unrelated to each other.

In general, the more tolerant people are of novelty, complexity, and insolubility, the more likely they are to succeed as managers in information-rich, ambiguous environment. They are less overwhelmed by these ambiguous circumstances.

Work Ethic Orientation:

This refers to the extent to which people are committed to work and involved in their activities. Extreme work ethic values could lead to traits of workoholism and workaholic people tend to give predominant interest to work which might lead to premature burnout and health problems such as hypertension, anxiety etc. Some individuals are highly work-oriented while others try to do the minimum that is necessary go get by without being fired on the job. The extremely work ethic oriented person gets greatly involved in the job and lives up to being described as 'living, eating and breathing the job'. Extreme work ethic values could lead to traits of 'workoholism' when work becomes to be considered as the only primary motive for living with very little outside interests.

Matching Personality and Job Types:

This refers to the extent to which people successfully match their personalities with their jobs. If there is a perfect relationship between the job and personality, the job satisfaction and production turnover among the employees will be significantly higher. John Holland present six personality types and proposes that the satisfaction and the propensity to leave a job depend on the degree to which people successfully match their personalities with a suitable occupational environment. Holland's typology of personality is given as below: Vocational Typology

Personality Characteristics
Congruent Occupations
Realistic
Shy, genuine, persistent,
Mechanic, drill press operator,
stable, conforming,
assembly- line worker, farmer
practical

Investigative
Analytical, original,
Biologists, economist,
curious, independent
mathematician, news reporter
Social
Sociable, friendly,

Social worker, teacher,
cooperative, understanding, counselor, clinical psychologists Conventional
Conforming, efficient,
Accountant, corporate manager,
practical, unimaginative,
bank teller, file clerk
inflexible
Enterprising
Self-confident, ambitious,
Lawyer, real estate agent, public
energetic, domineering
relations specialist, small
business manager
Artistic
Imaginative, disorderly,
Painter, musician, writer,
idealistic, emotional,
interior decorator
impractical

· **Realistic:** The type of activities for this category involves physical activities which require skill, strength and coordination. The suitable personality characteristics to meet these activities would be shy, genuine, persistent, stable, conforming, practical etc. The congruent occupations for this category of people are assembly line worker, farmer, mechanic etc.

· **Investigative:** The type of activities for this category involves thinking, organizing and understanding. The appropriate characteristics to meet these activities would be analytical, original, curious, independent etc. The congruent occupations for this category of people are biologists, economist, mathematician, news reporter.

· **Social:** The type of activities for this category involves helping and developing others. The relevant personality characteristics to meet these s activities would be sociable, friendly, cooperative, understanding. The congruent occupations for this category of people are social worker, teacher, counselor, clinical psychologists.

· **Conventional:** The type of activities for this category involves rule-regulated, orderly and unambiguous activities. The appropriate characteristics to these activities would be conforming, efficient, practical, unimaginative, and inflexible.

The congruent occupations for this category of people are accountant, corporate manager, and bank teller file clerk.

· **Enterprising:** The type of activist for this category involves verbal activities specific to influence others and attain power. The suitable personality characteristics to meet these activities would be self confident, ambitious, energetic, and domineering. The congruent occupations for this category of people are lawyer, real estate agent, public relations specialist, small business manager.

· **Artistic:** The type of activities for this category involves ambiguous and unsystematic activities that allow creative expression. The suitable personality characteristics to meet theses activities would be imaginative, disorderly, idealistic, emotional, and impractical. The congruent occupations are painter, musician, writer, interior decorator etc.

Holland's model proposes that a realistic person in a realistic jobs is in a more compatible situation than is a realistic person in an investigate job. Sociable person should be in social jobs, conventional people in convention jobs and so forth. Due care must be exercised to ensure a perfect between personality characteristics and the type of jobs offered to the candidates during the selection process. The person-organization fit essentially argues that people leave jobs that are not compatible with their personalities.

Most Common Defense Mechanisims

MOST COMMON DEFENSE MECHANISIMS	
Repression (The Primary Mechanism)	The person tries to banish offending desires from conscious thought to the point of being totally unaware of the original desires. *(Keeping distressing thoughts and feelings buried in the unconscious)*
Rationalization	The person attempts to deal with a stressful situation by claiming that the stressor was of minimal importance and may even have had beneficial effects. *(Creating false but plausible excuses to justify unacceptable behavior)*
Sublimation	The person *unconsciously* transforms conflict and anxiety into different but related desire that is more acceptable to society and to him/her self.
Identification	The person *attempts* to take on the virtues of an admired person. *(Bolstering self-esteem by forming an imaginary or real alliance with some person or group)*
Reaction Formation	The person *pretends* to possess desires that are the opposite if the desires that are causing conflict and anxiety. *(Behaving in a way that is exactly the opposite of one's true feelings)*
Projection	The person attributes to others the desires or thoughts that have caused personal conflict. *(attributing one's own thoughts, feelings, or motives to another)*
Denial	The person attempts to dispel anxiety by refusing altogether to accept reality.
Displacement Substitution Sublimination	The person tries to escape the discomfort of unwanted ideas or feelings by transferring them onto another person. *(diverting emotional feelings, usually anger, from their original source to a substitute target)*
Regression	The person retreats toward behaviors that usually characterize a lower level of maturity. *(a reversion to immature patterns of behavior)*
Introjection	Identifying with some idea or object so deeply that it becomes a part of that person. One example often used is when a child envelops representational images of his absent parents into himself, simultaneously fusing them with his own personality.
Compensation Direct Compensation Overcompensation	Encountering failure or frustration in some sphere of activity, one overemphasizes another. The term is also applied to the process of over-correcting for a handicap or limitation. Examples: (1) a physically unattractive adolescent becomes an expert dancer. (2) a youth with residual muscle damage from poliomyelitis becomes an athlete. (3) Demosthenes.
Intellectualization	(isolation). Concentrating on the intellectual components of the situations as to distance oneself from the anxiety provoking emotions associated with these situations. Intellectualization is a defense mechanism where reasoning is used to block confrontation with an unconscious conflict and its associated

	emotional stress. It involves removing one's self, emotionally, from a stressful event. Intellectualization is often accomplished through rationalization; rather than accepting reality, one may explain it away to remove one's self.
Fixation	Fixation in human psychology refers to the state where an individual becomes obsessed with an attachment to another human, animal or inanimate object

NEO-FREUDIAN THEORIES

Psychologists who concurred with Sigmund Freud and contributed to development of Freudian Psychoanalysis had differed from the approach of Freud in different aspects of explaining the nature of human being in different ways. Those psychologists are collectively known as Neo Freudian Psychologists. Prominent among the neo Freudians are Alfred Adler, Carl Jung, Erickson, Karen Horney, Erich Fromm, Harry Stack Sullivan, Anna Freud, and D.W.Winnicott.

Individual Psychology of Alfred Adler

Alfred Adler's psychological perspective is termed individual psychology. Adler emphasizes that an individual's thinking, feeling, emotion, and behavior can only be understood as subordinated to the individual's style of life, or consistent pattern of dealing with life. The personality remains to be one's style of life. It is not that an individual is internally divided or his mind remains the battleground of conflicting forces.

Each aspect of the personality points in the same direction. Hence personality is a holistic phenomenon. Adler emphasizes that an individual's thinking, feeling, emotion, and behavior can only be understood as subordinated to the individual's style of life, or consistent pattern of dealing with life. Adler holds that every one is born into the world with a sense of inferiority. An individual starts his course of life as a weak and helpless child and constantly strives to overcome these deficiencies by becoming superior to those around us. This process of struggling is designated as struggle a *striving for superiority.*

Striving for superiority remains the driving force behind all human thoughts, emotions, and behaviors.

Individuals strive to be accomplished writers, powerful business people, or influential politicians because of their feelings of inferiority and a strong need to over come this negative part of them. Some time the excessive feeling of inferiority can bring the opposite effect as well. When this feeling of inferiority becomes overwhelming and without being accompanied by the needed successes, an individual could develop an inferiority complex. Inferiority complex as a belief leaves in an individual feeling incredibly less important and deserving than others, helpless, hopeless, and unmotivated to strive for the superiority that would make us complete.

The parenting of children is a significant factor influencing the development of the child. Improper or inefficient child rearing has long-term effects on the child development. Two of the parental styles identified to exerting great effect on development of the child connotes papering and neglect. Pampering, a parent overprotecting a child, giving him too much attention, and sheltering him from the negative realities of life might lead a child to grow ill equipped to deal with these realities, developing doubt about his own abilities or decision making skills, and to constantly seeking out others to replace the safety he once enjoyed as a child. A neglected child not protected at all from the world and forced to face life's struggles alone may grow up to fear the world, have a strong sense of mistrust for others and she may have a difficult time forming intimate relationships. Properly balanced parental style may protect children form the evils of the world but not shelter them from it. Such a style would envisage parents to allowing the child to hear or see the negative aspects of the world while still feeling the safety of parental influence. Parent who follows the proper parental style may not immediately rush to the school authorities if his child is getting bullied; rather he would teach his child how to respond or take care of oneself at school.

The order in which an individual is born to a family inherently affects his or her personality. The first-born children who later have younger siblings may have the worst effect on their personality. They are given excessive attention and pampering by their parents until when the little sibling is born. They find everything is changed suddenly and they are no longer the center of attention and fall into the shadows. Such children are left feeling inferior, questioning their importance in the family, and trying desperately to gain back the attention they suddenly lost. The theory of birth order theory suggests that first-born children often have the greatest number of problems, as they get older.

Middle born children may have their personality inspired by their position of birth in the family. They are not pampered as their older sibling was, but are still afforded the attention of the parents. As a middle child, an individual may have the luxury of trying to dethrone the oldest child and become more superior while at the same time knowing that he or she holds the same power over their younger siblings. Thus, middle children develop and have a high need for superiority and are often able to seek it out such as through healthy competition.

Children born as the youngest children, like the first born, may be more likely to experience personality problems later in life. This is because the youngest born child who grows up knowing that he has the least amount of power in the whole family. The youngest born may see his older siblings as having more freedom and more superiority.

The youngest born is also gets pampered and protected more than any other child did.

Such experiences could leave the youngest born individual with a sense that he cannot take on the world alone and that will always be inferior to others.

Analytical Psychology of Carl J Jung

The psychological perspectives of Carl Jung are termed analytical psychology. Jung disagreed with the Freudian formulation of the construct of unconscious. He was conceived that there were fears, behaviors, and thoughts that children and adults exhibit that are remarkably similar across time and culture and similarity witnessed was more than coincidence. He propounded the concept of *collective unconscious* to account for the witnessed similarity across time and culture. Jung stresses that it the collective unconscious that influences the personality. It is generally agreed among the critics that Jung has pieced together an important, and previously missing, explanation of these personality aspects that we all share.

The collective unconscious is made up of archetypes which are *primordial images* inherited from our ancestors. The immediate attachment infants have for their mother, the inevitable fear of the dark seen in young children, and how images such as the sun, moon, wise old man, angels, and evil all seem to be predominate themes throughout history lend credence to the existence of collective unconscious. Infants are drawn to their mother because of the unconscious image of mother that is alive in all human beings and every child fears the dark because of the unconscious image of darkness.

Of the archetypes described by Jung a few including the animus/anima, the shadow, and the self have more application in personality theory. The masculine side of the female is terms animus and the feminine side of the male is called the anima. Unlike Freud who believed that individuals are all born bisexual and develop normal sexual attraction through our psychosexual development, Jung remained convinced that every one has an unconscious opposite gender hidden within him or herself and the role of this archetype is to guide individual toward the perfect mate. In other words, people project our animus/anima onto others as they project theirs on to us: when a match is made, people have found a suitable partner.

The shadow is basically the unconscious negative or dark side of one's personality. The shadow, like all other archetypes, is passed down through history and given different names depending on time and culture. The self-archetype is the unifying part of all the people that finds balance in the lives of the people. Working with the ego which is partly in our personal unconscious, may help manage the other archetypes and helps one feel complete.

CONFLICT PROCESS

The conflict process can be categorized into five stages. They are as follows:

Stage I: Potential opposition or incompatibility:

This covers the present condition that creates opportunity for conflicts to arise. This may be one of the conditions responsible for the occurrence of conflict. The major sources of conflict can be further categorized as communication, structure and personal variables.

Communication: It is reported that word connotations, jargon, insufficient exchange of information and noise in the communication channel are all barriers to communication and potential antecedent conditions to conflict.

Structure: It is reported that the size and specialization act as forces to stimulate conflict.

The larger the group size and the more specialized its activities, the greater the likihood of conflict. The potential for conflict tend to be greatest when group members are younger and when turnover is high.

Personal variables: The evidence indicates that certain personality types such as highly authoritarian and dogmatic people who demonstrate low self-esteem lead to potential conflicts.

Stage II: Cognition and personalization:

Perception or sense making plays a major role in the resolving conflict. Conflict may either be perceived or felt in nature. Perceived conflict is defined as awareness by one or more parties of the existence of conditions that create opportunities for conflict to arise.

Felt conflict is defined as emotional involvement in a conflict creating anxiety, tenseness, frustrations or hostility. Negative emotions have been found to produce over simplification of issues, reductions in trust, and negative interpretations of the other party's behavior.

Stage III: Intentions:

Using two dimensions – cooperativeness (the degree to which one party attempts to satisfy the other party's concerns) and assertiveness (the degree to which one party attempts to satisfy his or her own concerns) – five conflict handling intentions can be identified. There are as follows: i) competing (assertive and uncooperative), ii) collaborating (assertive and cooperative), iii) avoiding (unassertive and uncooperative), iv) accommodating (unassertive and cooperative) and v) compromising (mid-range on both assertiveness and cooperativeness).

Stage IV: Behavior:

All conflicts manifest in behavior somewhere along with continuum ranging from no conflict or minor conflict such as minor disagreements or misunderstanding, overt questioning or challenging of others, to annihilatory conflict such as threats and ultimatum, aggressive physical attacks or overt efforts to destroy the other party.

Stage V: Outcomes.

The outcomes of conflict may be functional or dysfunctional. Conflict is constructive when it improves the quality of decision, stimulates creativity and innovation, encourages interest and curiosity among group members, provides the medium through which problems can be aired and tensions released and fosters an environment of self-evaluation and change. The evidence suggest that conflict can improve the quality of decision making allowing all points particularly the ones that are unusual or held by a minority people. The dysfunctional consequences of conflict on a group or organization's performance are generally well known. Among the more undesirable consequences are retarding of communication, reduction in group cohesiveness and subordination of group goals to the primacy of infighting between members. At the extreme, conflict can bring group functioning to a halt and potentially threaten the group's survival.

TYPES OF CONFLICT

In organizations, conflicts can be interpersonal, intra- group, inter-group or intra-organizational in nature. Intra-organizational conflict encompasses vertical, horizontal, line-staff and role conflict.

Vertical Conflict:

It refers to conflicts that occur between individuals at different levels. Conflict between the superior and subordinate is an example of vertical conflict. Such conflicts could happen because of perceived transgression of psychological contract, inadequate or ineffective communication, selective perception, misperception, incongruence in goals, values, cognition, affect and behavior etc.

Horizontal Conflict:

It refers to tensions between employees or groups at the same hierarchical level. Horizontal conflict occurs because of interdependence among the parties concerned in the work situation or the common pooled resources shared. For example, sharing personal computers among the various departments is likely to produce tensions among the departments. Incompatibility of goal and time orientations often results in horizontal conflicts. Conflicts will take place between the units due to the misunderstanding and frustration experienced by both parties. Horizontal conflict increases as: i) functional interdependence increasers among people or groups at the same level ii) more units depend on common resources that have to be shared raw materials and iii) the fewer the buffers or inventories for the resources shared.

Line and Staff Conflict:

It refers to the conflicts that arise between those who assist or act in an advisory capacity (staff) and those who have direct authority to create the products, process, and services of the organizing (line). Staff managers and line managers usually have different personality predispositions and goals and come from different backgrounds. Staff managers have specialized skills and expertise acquired through training and education and have greater technical knowledge which is intended to help the line manager who are basically money maker for the organization. Staff people serve as advisor for the line people in as much as they have the expertise to streamline methods and help in cost-cutting mechanisms. Line managers may feel that the staff people are unnecessarily interfering in their work by always telling them how to do their job and thrusting their ideas and methods. Staff people often get frustrated that the line people do not consider all the ideas put forth by them and thereby fail to benefit.

Role Conflict:

It arises because different people in the organization are expected to perform different task and pressures build up when the expectation of the members clash in several ways.

There are two types of conflict.

i) Inter-sender role conflict: This occurs when different role senders (bosses) expect the individual to perform different things and these expectations and the messages conflict with each other

ii) Inter-role conflict: This occurs when role requires associated with members in one group conflicts with role requirements stemming from members in another group.

INTRODUCTION TO SOCIAL WORK

(SYLLABUS AND STUDY MATERIAL)

PROJECT MSW,
DEPARTMENT OF SOCIAL WORK,
PSG COLLEGE OF ARTS AND SCIENCE, COIMBATORE,
COPRIGHT BELONGS TO ALL STUDENT OF SOCIAL WORK DEPARTMENT
(2012 – 2014 BATCH)
CREATOR: T.M.SURESH
CONTENT CREATOR: G.SANTHOSH
CONTRIBUTERS: THIVYA VILASHINI
AND ALL MSW STUDENTS

SYLLABUS

Unit – I   SOCIAL WORK

Concept – definition of social work – principles and process of social work. Role of social workers – the concept of social services and welfare in relation to social work – social work as a profession – social work values – code and ethics.

Unit – II HISTORICAL DEVELOPMENT

Historical background of social work U.S.A & India – contribution of religious and reform movements for social change and social welfare. Social work – social work education in India – professionalization of social work education.

Unit – III METHODS OF SOCIAL WORK

 A brief understanding of methods of social work – social case work – social group work – community organization – social work research – social action – social welfare administration.

Unit – IV FIELDS OF SOCIAL WORK

Social work practice in industry – hospitals – correctional settings – social settings – social work through non - governmental organizations.

Unit – V RECENT TRENDS

Field work and its importance to social work education – transactional analysis for social work practice – the concept of integrated social work approach – the problems and prospects of the profession – the future of social work.

Unit – I   SOCIAL WORK

Concept – definition of social work – principles and process of social work. Role of social workers – the concept of social services and welfare in relation to social work – social work as a profession – social work values – code and ethics.

DEFNITION OF SOCIAL WORK:

                              Social work may be defined as an art, a science, and a profession that helps people to solve personal, group, and community problem and attain satisfying personal, group, and community relationships through social work practice.

PRINCIPLES:

- ☐   A problem exists everywhere
- ☐   Every person is unique and environment has an effect on the person
- ☐   Any situation can be changed
- ☐   Trained social worker
- ☐   It is professional
- ☐   Social work is possible to some extent only with community cooperation.

A fundamental, well-settled accepted tenets. A basic truth or undisputed doctrine; a given proposition that is clear and does not need to be proved. It is basically a hypothesis, an assumption so adequately tested by observation / experience / experiment may be used as a guide for action, or as a means of understanding. Konapka (1958), Clarke (1947), Cohen (1958), Friedlander (1958), Perlman (1976) Piccard (1988), Morales & Sheafor (1998) explained about Social Work Principles.

1. **Principle of Acceptance**. Acceptance originate from Greek word "agape" which means "love which descends to misery, ugliness and guilt in order to elevate. The love is critical and is able to transform what it loves. This love (acceptance is not charity) is not charity which is an escape from the demands of critical love acceptance penetrates to the inner selves of others and affirms their humanity

2. **Principle of Individualization** Social Workers by their training develop a generalized understanding of people, their problems and their environment. If one applies this to all it may lead to bias, prejudice, labeling, stereotyping and ignoring the beauty of diversity and uniqueness. This principle emphasis that client (group / Community) have a right "to be individuals and be treated not as a human being but as this human being with personal differences…and this transformed into "start where the client / group /community is"

3. **Principle of Purposeful Expression of Feeling** / Principle of Meaningful Relationship / Principle of Controlled Emotional Involvement … Principle of Empathy

3. **Purposeful Expression of Feeling Social workers have to go beyond the content of just the facts to uncover feelings that underlie these facts. By listening attentively, asking relevant questions and demonstrating tolerance and non judgmentalism social workers encourage clients to share their feelings** …to relieve pressure or tension. A cathartic or cleansing experience that enable clients to put their situation in perspective.

Empathy Putting oneself into the psychological frame of reference of another, so that the other person's feeling, thinking, and acting are understood and to some extent predictable. A desirable trust-building characteristic of a helping profession. It is embodied in the sincere statement, "I understand how you feel." Empathy is different from sympathy in that to be empathetic one understands how the person feels rather than actually experiencing those feelings, as in sympathy.

How we call a person with little or no empathy? Anyone with a high level of the trait of narcissism (an inflated self-esteem, a sense of superiority and a feeling of entitlement) generally has little empathy or sympathy for others.

Controlled Emotional Involvement Controlled emotional involvement is in no sense a "hardening" process. It is rather a mellowing process which serves to steady and temper our emotional responses. Over identification with clients impedes objectivity and neutrality.

Meaningful Relationship Meaningful relationship begins by demonstrating the interests in client.

4. **Principle of Non Judgmental Attitude Non judge mentalism presumes acceptance.** Nonjudgmental social work excludes assigning guilt or innocence, or degree of client responsibility for causation of the problems or needs but it does include making evaluative judgments about the attitudes and standards or actions of the client. Non judge mentalism signifies social workers' non blaming attitudes and behaviors…not judging clients as good or bad, or worthy or unworthy.

5. Principle of Objectivity It is closely related to non-judge mentalism

6. **Principle of Self Determination** Positively it means having freedom to make mistakes as well as to act wisely. Negatively not being coerced or manipulated. Self-determination acknowledges that sound growth emanates from within.

7. Principle of Confidentiality Confidential means private or secret; something treated with trust, resulting in a feeling of security that information will not be disclosed to other parties. An example is the confidentiality of conversations and records between attorney and client.

8. **Principle of Accountability**

9. **Principle of Access to Resources**

PROCESS OF SOCIAL WORKER:

- ☐ Intake

- ☐ Study

- ☐ Social Diagnosis (analyzing a problem)

- ☐ Treatment

  - Support

  - Clarification

  - Insight (Root cause of a problem)

  - Identification   (Finding an actual problem maker)

  - Resources utilization

- Evaluation (To check our progress whether we are going in a correct way)

- Environmental modification

☐ Rehabitation (to help the person to come to a normal life after treatment)

ROLE OF SOCIAL WORKER:

Often students get confused between the services of the aforementioned professions and those of "counselors." Counseling can be done by psychic- trysts, psychologists, and social workers, as well as guidance counselors and clergy. Counseling is a broader category than the previously discussed disciplines. Many people get jobs as counselors, yet the required education, experience, and licensing varies considerably among these positions. Some require no licensing and only minimal education. And, as discussed, psychiatrists, psychologists, and social workers providing counseling services require many years of education and experience. Some counselors deal with mental health, while other counselors help people with their educational and career concerns. For example, mental health counselors help individuals with problems such as suicide, stress, and drug and alcohol addictions. Rehabilitation counselors, in contrast, help individuals with vocational needs affected by disabilities. These disabilities may be physical, mental, or social. Counselors work not only with individuals but often with the families of those individuals. In any case, counseling positions normally require one to two years of graduate study, a master's degree in a specific discipline, and supervised counseling experience. As previously discussed, requirements for licensing and certification vary depending upon specialty and state. A major requirement in many social work jobs, therefore, is collaboration with a number of professionals from various disciplines, perspectives, and educational experiences. This collaboration, often in the form of partnerships, coalitions, or interdisciplinary teams, is becoming more and more important. Recent conservative social welfare policy, as well as the demands of managed care, has resulted in fewer resources for agencies in the social welfare system. This often results in limited services, more short- term interventions, and more narrow eligibility requirements for services. In an effort to provide comprehensive care, health and human service agencies are forced to collaborate in helping to solve individual and social problems. This collaboration can result in increased resources and expertise, thereby helping social workers and other professionals better address the multidimensional problems of individuals, families, and communities. Collaboration also requires better integrated services, which avoids service duplication and service gaps. Consequently, many funders of health and human services today require community agencies to collaborate to receive grants for service provision.

That service to others is more important than self-interest, the dominant value of the market economy. A second core value is social justice. Much of what social workers do involves social and economic justice. Social workers promote social change with and on behalf of vulnerable populations—groups such as women, racial and ethnic minorities, children, and people with disabilities. To accomplish this, social workers strive to develop more just policies, programs, and services for these groups in need. (Note: By "racial and ethnic minorities," we mean groups that, based on their race or ethnicity, are rendered subordinate to society's more dominant groups. More information on this topic will be provided in Chapter 5.) They also emphasize "human rights" such as freedom, privacy, safety, education, health care, and decent standards of living. The aforementioned groups often suffer from social problems, including poverty, discrimination, unemployment, and oppression. Often these are groups that are either too young or too old to participate in the market or, because of race or gender, have been discriminated against in their efforts to participate in the market economy. Social workers, therefore, work to promote more just and humane policies as well as programs to address these issues. Another core value in social work is the dignity and worth of each per- son. All social workers must respect the inherent dignity and worth of every individual. This is a prerequisite for developing effective helping relationships with individuals, families, and groups. In the process, social workers need to understand the unique cultures and backgrounds of the people with whom they work. This requires an openness and sensitivity to the unique experiences of every individual. It also involves the promotion of self-determination for each individual. A fourth core value of social work is the importance of human relation- ships. One reason for this is that social workers use human relationships to promote change in individuals, families, groups, and communities. Social workers also understand that helping people to develop healthy human relationships is a means to a high-quality life and happiness for all people. Healthy human relationships are a prerequisite for meeting the needs of love and belonging and for developing healthy families. Integrity is a fifth basic value in social work. Professional social workers must act with integrity at all times. In so doing, social workers develop the trust of clients and coworkers. Social workers also work to promote ethical policies and practices in the organizations in which they are employed. Furthermore, integrity is an important factor for social workers if they are to have the credibility needed to promote social justice. A final core value of the social work profession is competence. Social workers must practice within the areas of their competence and must continually work to develop and enhance their professional expertise. What is more, social workers should look for opportunities to contribute to the profession's knowledge base through education, scientific inquiry, and evaluation of programs and their individual practice.

Social Work in Relation to Social Welfare
The profession of social work has developed within the context of the United States' social welfare system. Pioneering social workers could be found in 19th-century institutions such as settlement houses and charity organization societies. Today, the social welfare system, by definition, refers to our nation's system of programs, benefits, and services that help people meet those social, economic, educational, and health needs that are fundamental to the maintenance of society. These programs and services, primarily located in the public and private nonprofit sectors of U.S. society, include Social Security, unemployment insurance, and workers ' compensation, Temporary Assistance to Needy Families, food stamps, public housing, Medicare, and Medicaid. Our social welfare system also includes Alcoholics Anonymous (AA) support groups, Mothers against Drunk Driving, the YMCA, the Girl Scouts of America, and Habitat for Humanity, the American Red Cross, the Salvation Army, United Way, local faith-based services, and other voluntary associations in the private nonprofit sector.

A more detailed discussion of social welfare in relation to social work will be provided in Chapter 3. But for now, the reader should remember that social welfare is a broader concept than social work. Most social workers are employed in the U.S. social welfare system. Social work is a profession; social welfare is a "system" that employs many professions. That is, professionals from many other fields also practice within the social welfare system, including people from fields such as public administration, law, nursing, sociology, psychology, and medicine. Social workers frequently collaborate with these other professionals when assisting clients. In any case, students interested in social work have a wide variety of jobs from which to choose.

Social work as a profession:
The term profession thus refers to an occupation, vocation or high-status career, usually involving prolonged academic training, formal qualifications and membership of a professional or regulatory body. Professions involve the application of specialized knowledge of a subject, field, or science to fee-paying clientele. It is axiomatic that "professional activity involves systematic knowledge and proficiency. "Professions are usually regulated by professional bodies that may set examinations of competence, act as a licensing authority for practitioners, and enforce adherence to an ethical code of practice. Contents

1 .Examples of the professions
 2 Formation of a profession
3. Regulations
4. Autonomy
5. Status and prestige
6. Power
7. History
8. Gender inequality
9. racial inequality
10. Characteristics of a profession

Social workers involved in casework with individuals work in a wide variety of practice settings, including social service agencies, hospitals, outpatient clinics, state and local child protective services, and private practices. Social workers practicing casework with individuals include clinicians in an inpatient psychiatric facility, case managers in a residential shelter for homeless youth, social workers working with dialysis patients in a hospital, and adult protective service workers. Case management is similar to casework. Case management is defined as a service done by "an individual or team of professionals who organize, coordinate, and sustain a network of formal and informal supports in order to optimize the functioning and well-being of people with multiple needs."11 Because of their multiple needs, these people typically need several types of supports. It is the job of the case manager or member of an interdisciplinary case management team to link their client with all needed services and supports to which the client is entitled. In other words, case managers plan, seek, and monitor needed services from one or more agencies on behalf of a client. In so doing, the case manager may play several roles, including that of a broker, mediator, or advocate. Case management makes it easier for an individual client to locate services in a social service system that is often complex and fragmented. Consequently, case managers require a detailed knowledge of the full range of services at the com- munity level as well as a working knowledge of state and national services. Be that as it may, some social work students may be primarily interested in working with families in the future. For these students, the profession of social work holds many opportunities!

Social workers practice their profession in many different types of settings. Many work in the public sector. Many also work in the private nonprofit sector, while other social workers work in the private for-profit sector. Public sector jobs include those in federal, state, county, and local government agencies. Typical jobs in government settings include child protection, adoption, adult protection, veterans' services, public schools, and the correctional sys- tem. Private nonprofit jobs include those in health and human services such as the Boys and Girls Clubs, Meals on Wheels, the YMCA, the YWCA, the Red Cross, Big Brothers/Big Sisters, substance abuse prevention services, family counseling agencies, parent education and support services, and various advocacy organizations. The private for-profit sector is better known as the "business sector." Social workers find jobs in businesses in employee assistance programs, community relations, public affairs, corporate charitable contribution programs, and volunteer management programs. Social workers also work independently in private practice. In this case, social workers set up a proprietary practice that may involve consultation, research, educational workshops, and other non-clinical services. Many other social workers in private practice set up clinically oriented practices, usually providing mental health services. In any case, social workers in private practice need to be licensed, certified, or registered in accordance with state laws.

Social Work with Individuals

Depending upon the setting, many social workers provide services primarily to individual people. Social workers focused on work with individuals might provide case management, psychotherapy, and/or advocacy—usually all three. Social work with individuals has historically been referred to as "casework" or "social casework." Casework, by definition, involves the use of social work knowledge, values, and skills in face-to-face relationships to resolve or reduce difficulties "arising out of disequilibrium between people and their environment."10 This process involves helping people adjust to their environment, as well as intervening to change factors in the individual's environment. Casework with individuals includes helping people with concrete practical problems, with environmental deficits and pressures, and with interpersonal and intrapersonal difficulties.

Social Work with Families

Social work with families became a distinct field in social work practice beginning in the 1960s. Social workers who work with families help family members improve their patterns of interaction to better meet the needs of all family members.13 In other words, social workers aim to help families with behavioral, emotional, and interactional problems. The process is usually viewed as one of problem solving within a system's context—the system in this case being the family. At times, families develop dysfunctional coalitions and alliances within the family system. Social workers, sometimes employed in agencies as "family therapists," help families to change problematic family structures, leading not only to positive transformation of the family, but positive change in each of the family members as well. Social workers who work with families draw from a number of different theories about how families work and how families change. In doing so, social workers may use a number of techniques and play a number of roles.

Some may focus on specific relationships, such as that between a between a parent and child, or may extend their work to include a range of extended family. Sometimes they videotape family members interacting during the therapeutic session. Sometimes one-way mirrors are used so that family interactional pat- terns can be observed by other family members. In addition, role-playing may be used where family members are asked to reenact prior conflicts. Sometimes a therapist acts as a model of more functional behavior when dealing with conflict. This may include ways to communicate more effectively. At other times, social workers doing family therapy perform the educator role in an effort to better inform family members regarding strategies for improved family relationships. Furthermore, social workers working with families frequently attempt to link these families to community resources in an effort to provide additional or long-term support to the family. This may entail referring families to parenting programs, support groups, 12-step groups such as AA and Al-Anon, affordable housing, transportation services, or anger management classes. Such referrals may result from the social worker collaborating with other professionals—psychologists, nurses, and so on—in an inter disciplinary team.14 While some social work students may want to work with families, other students may be interested in working with a wider variety of groups. They see themselves in some aspect of "group work."

Social Work with Groups

Although group work as an intervention method in social work can be traced back to the settlement houses and mutual aid societies of the late 1800s in America, it became recognized as a distinct professional intervention method within social work in the 1930s. Group work or social group work as a social work intervention method is defined as an intervention that utilizes group process, based in large part on social systems theory, to promote positive change among group members. This process is typically goal-directed around common interests of group members. These interests may include common emotional problems, educational needs, skill development, or recreational opportunities.15 Consider the following examples. When working with individuals, social workers use groups to provide support to people who are coping with a common issue, such as the loss of a loved one or the diagnosis of a disease. At times, groups are used to educate clients around such issues as parenting or substance abuse prevention. Sometimes the groups are therapy groups that help group members with rehabilitation of a serious personal problem such as depression or violent anger. Many groups run by social workers incorporate both educational and behavior change components, such as groups designed to help individuals with diabetes improve their diet, teenagers avoid pregnancy and STDs, or college students reduce their stress level. These groups are often referred to as "psycho educational" groups. Sometimes groups are used to address functional deficits, as with adolescents needing social and problem-solving skills. At other times, social workers use groups in a purely developmental sense, such as recreation groups, arts and crafts groups, reading groups, consciousness- raising groups, team-building groups, staff development groups, or other types of empowerment groups.

Social Work with Communities

Social workers who work with communities are often called "community organizers." In this instance, the client is the community and the intervention process is called "community organization." Community organization is defined by its use of planned collective action to address the needs of people from the same geographic area or with some other common interests. The intervention typically involves community needs assessment and the development of community leaders, action strategies, and required resources to address unmet needs. To illustrate, the community need may be less crime, better schools, cleaner streets, or improved recreational facilities. Sometimes the need is greater economic opportunity, in which case social workers may get involved in planning for economic development within the community. In any case, social workers working as community organizers facilitate collective action in an effort to promote positive community change. Social workers working to better community well-being perform a variety of tasks. They could help to establish a neighborhood organization. They may organize a meeting to discuss problems with neighborhood youth. They might help community residents establish a buyers club to purchase low-cost heating oil. Further, social workers may assist communities in planning and conducting neighborhood fairs and festivals that celebrate national holidays or the ethnic heritage of community members. Social workers in the community organization role might also help residents raise funds from local businesses to build better playgrounds for neigh- boyhood children. Some may organize peaceful demonstrations for improved city services to the neighborhood. Whatever the case, the goal of communityorganization is greater well-being for the residents of the community. Working to better meet the needs of communities is great for some, but other social workers enjoy running organizations. Consequently, they seek administrative positions.

Social Workers in Administration

Many career paths lead social workers into administration. Frequently, these are social workers who concentrated on the more macro aspects of the profession while in school. Often administrative social workers find employment in private nonprofit agencies as Chief Executive Officers (CEOs), executive directors, or program directors. Many also find work in government agencies as heads of various government divisions, program directors, or even commissioners of entire departments. Social workers at the top levels of management are responsible for many administrative tasks. For example, they ensure their agency conducts regular strategic planning, which often involves community needs assessment. They oversee program development, which includes program design, fundraising, and program evaluation. Social administrators are responsible for staff development, including hiring, evaluation, and termination. Social administrators are also involved in policy advocacy and community education as well as interagency collaboration. Administrators of private nonprofit agencies assist with board development for their organizations. This typically includes working with existing board members to recruit and train new board members. Social workers in nonprofit management, given the importance of volunteers in nonprofit organizations, must also take responsibility for recruiting, developing, and managing volunteers. In addition, nonprofit administrators spend a great deal of their time in fund-raising. Funds are raised in many ways. Vehicles for fund-raising include grant writing, grass-roots events such as walkathons and road races, annual campaigns to solicit individual donations, planned giving involving bequests, and capital campaigns to raise money for the development of new facilities. Social workers who go into administrative practice often enjoy developing and administering new programs to meet emerging community needs. Given their macro perspective, they like working with larger systems. And they enjoy collaboration, coordination, and leadership. But if you have a macro perspective, yet don't want administrative responsibilities, maybe social welfare policy development would be a better match for you.

Social Workers in Policy Practice

Social welfare policy defines the context in which social services are developed and delivered. Many social workers, particularly those who concentrated in macro practice as students, find employment in policy practice.17 Policy practice in social work, by definition, involves the formulation, enactment, implementation, and assessment of social welfare policies. While some social workers in policy practice hold elected offices, social workers more often find jobs as policy planners or policy analysts. Some work for elected officials or in government agencies at the national, state, or local levels, while many others work in private nonprofit agencies, especially large nonprofit agencies at the national and state levels, agencies such as the Children's Defense fund, the Child Welfare League of America, or United Way of America. Social workers' firsthand knowledge of the needs of various client populations is highly valued by policymakers in national, state, and local government. Social workers engaged in policy work carry out a variety of specific tasks. They help to define social problems, analyze the values underlying such problem definitions, set policy goals and objectives in relation to the problems, outline policy options for achieving these goals and objectives, consider various criteria for evaluating policy options, and ultimately, decide on final policy proposals to advocate and implement. Social workers involved with policy development sometimes are only involved in the research and analysis that goes into developing proposals, while at other times they make direct recommendations as to which policy options they consider best. This is because social workers' knowledge of how health and human services are produced, distributed, and consumed is critical to the policy development process.18 For this and other reasons, social workers in policy practice enjoy the opportunity to develop and influence policies that affect many people. If policy practice as well as case work, group work, and community organization are not for you, social work offers employment in still another area: research.

Social Workers in Research
Social workers engage in research for several reasons. They identify research- based interventions to achieve client goals. They also use research to evaluate program outcomes and practice effectiveness. For example, social welfare policies typically result in social welfare programs and services that then need to be evaluated as one step in determining the success or failure of the original legislation. Social workers in administration are typically responsible for seeing that program evaluations are done, and social workers frequently conduct these evaluations of programs and services. What is more, some social workers earn a Ph.D. and gain employment at universities in teaching and research. These social work educators utilize their practice experience to inform their research—and ultimately, their students! Okay, so we have established that social workers do many things. But what, you may wonder, makes social work different from psychology and sociology and other fields? We address this question in the following section.

Social Work in Relation to Other Professions
Social work is a profession within the social welfare system. As such, social workers apply scientific knowledge and technical skills to assist their clients. More specifically, social work is a professional activity focused on helping individuals, groups, organizations, and communities enhance or restore their capacity for social functioning. Social workers also strive to create societal conditions conducive to these goals. In so doing, social work requires knowledge of human development and behavior, societal institutions, and the interaction between individuals and larger institutional systems. In other words, social work focuses on three things: the person, the system, and the relation- ship between the person and the system.20 often when individuals have problems, these are the result of dysfunctional transactions between the person and his or her environment. Social workers are trained to focus on these transactions. In carrying out their interventions, social workers apply various theories. Foremost among them are systems theory and ecological theory (to be discussed in more detail in Chapter 2). Systems theory suggests that no problem can be fully understood by breaking it down into component parts. The relationship among the various parts of the whole system is as important as each part individually. Most systems seek a balance in an effort to maintain and preserve the system, whether that system is a family, a group, or a community. Problems arise when systems experience an imbalance due to any number of factors. Similarly, the ecological perspective, or "ecosystems perspective," stresses that human beings develop and adapt to transactions with all elements in their environmental systems. Based in part on these theories, social work intervention emphasizes a focus on the person in his or her environment.21 because social workers work in the social welfare system, they collaborate with professionals from other disciplines. These professional disciplines tend to have slightly different perspectives regarding people and their environments. These related disciplines include sociology, psychology, and psychiatry. Sociology is the study of the origins, organizations, institutions, and development of human society. When going about their work, sociologists, who typically have five to seven years of graduate study, attempt to explain the ways in which human societies influence individual functioning within those societies. In addition, sociologists attempt to understand the differences among various human societies. Therefore, sociologists seek to understand, for example, the effect of living in a market economy on individual behavior, the effect of democratic institutions on individual behavior, the influence of racist institutions on individual functioning, and the effect of urbanization on human development. A psychologist, in contrast, studies human behavior and mental process- es in an effort to understand human behavior for individual functioning. That is, psychology is the study of mental processes and behavior. Because psychologists study mind and behavior, professionals in this discipline are interested in the function of the brain, child development, and, in general, "what makes people tick." Psychologists often specialize in certain areas, including clinical psychology, counseling, developmental psychology, or social psychology. Each of these specializations examines a different aspect of human behavior. Psychologists who specialize in clinical psychology often work in hospitals, clinics, and private practice. They often use inter-viewing techniques, diagnostic tests, and psychotherapy in their practice. Psychologists with a master's degree are able to administer and interpret tests, counsel patients, and conduct research. A Ph.D. in psychology typically requires five to seven years of graduate study and two years of professional experience for certification or licensure. Licensure requirements vary from state to state. Psychiatry is the study of the diagnosis, treatment, and prevention of mental illness. In

other words, psychiatrists specialize in the problem of mental illness. In so doing, psychiatrists work in private practice, in courtrooms, and in specialized medical settings such as coronary and intensive care units. In addition, they often serve as consultants to other agencies. Psychiatrists are medical doctors, requiring five to seven additional years of psychiatric training and experience. As a result, they are qualified to use the full range of medical techniques related to mental illness. Such techniques include medication, shock, and surgery, as well as counseling and behavior modification. Psychiatrists generally use a medical model, which views the individual's problem as a disease or sickness that needs to be cured. Utilizing the medical model, psychiatrists typically examine symptoms in an effort to make a diagnosis. Once the diagnosis is made, psychiatrists prescribe the treatment with the highest likelihood of curing the disease or sickness. In contrast to the social worker's dual perspective of the "person-in-environment," in psychiatry, the individual's problem is considered to be inside the individual. In other words, in contrast to examining the person's environment for factors contributing to the problem, psychiatrists tend to focus on other possible contributing factors, including genetic endowment, metabolic disorders, unconscious defense mechanisms, childhood traumatic experiences, or infectious disease. Psychiatrists believe that the individual's mind has been negatively affected by one or more of these factors. Psychiatrists, being medical doctors, view people seeking their services as patients and provide "treatment" of the patient's problem. Often students get confused between the services of the aforementioned professions and those of "counselors." Counseling can be done by psychiatrists, psychologists, and social workers, as well as guidance counselors and clergy. Counseling is a broader category than the previously discussed disciplines. Many people get jobs as counselors, yet the required education, experience, and licensing varies considerably among these positions. Some require no licensing and only minimal education. And, as discussed, psychiatrists, psychologists, and social workers providing counseling services require many years of education and experience. Some counselors deal with mental health, while other counselors help people with their educational and career concerns. For example, mental health counselors help individuals with problems such as suicide, stress, and drug and alcohol addictions. Rehabilitation counselors, in contrast, help individuals with vocational needs affected by disabilities. These disabilities may be physical, mental, or social. Counselors work not only with individuals but often with the families of those individuals. In any case, counseling positions normally require one to two years of graduate study, a master's degree in a specific discipline, and supervised counseling experience. As previously discussed, requirements for licensing and certification vary depending upon specialty and state. A major requirement in many social work jobs, therefore, is collaboration with a number of professionals from various disciplines, perspectives, and educational experiences. This collaboration, often in the form of partnerships, coalitions, or interdisciplinary teams, is becoming more and more important. Recent conservative social welfare policy, as well as the demands of managed care, has resulted in fewer resources for agencies in the social welfare system. This often results in limited services, more short-term interventions, and more narrow eligibility requirements for services. In an effort to provide comprehensive care, health and human service agencies are forced to collaborate in helping to solve individual and social problems. This collaboration can result in increased resources and expertise, thereby helping social workers and other professionals better address the multidimensional problems of individuals, families, and communities. Collaboration also requires better integrated services, which avoids service duplication and service gaps. Consequently, many funders of health and human services today require community agencies to collaborate to receive grants for service provision.

Social work Values
Now that you have a better idea of what social workers do in their field, let's take a closer look at the profession's ideological foundation. The profession of social work is based upon a set of core values. These values are service, social justice, the dignity and worth of the person, the importance of human relation- ships, integrity, and competence.26 In terms of service, the primary goal of social work is to help people in need and to address social problems. This is the reason that many people choose to become social workers. Social workers believe that service to others is more important than self-interest, the dominant value of the market economy. A second core value is social justice. Much of what social workers do involves social and economic justice.

Social workers promote social change with and on behalf of vulnerable populations—groups such as women, racial and ethnic minorities, children, and people with disabilities. To accomplish this, social workers strive to develop more just policies, programs, and services for these groups in need. (Note: By "racial and ethnic minorities," we mean groups that, based on their race or ethnicity, are rendered subordinate to society's more dominant groups. More information on this topic will be provided in Chapter 5.) They also emphasize "human rights" such as freedom, privacy, safety, education, health care, and decent standards of living. The aforementioned groups often suffer from social problems, including poverty, discrimination, unemployment, and oppression. Often these are groups that are either too young or too old to participate in the market or, because of race or gender, have been discriminated against in their efforts to participate in the market economy. Social workers, therefore, work to promote more just and humane policies as well as programs to address these issues. Another core value in social work is the dignity and worth of each per- son. All social workers must respect the inherent dignity and worth of every individual. This is a prerequisite for developing effective helping relationships with individuals, families, and groups. In the process, social workers need to understand the unique cultures and backgrounds of the people with whom they work. This requires an openness and sensitivity to the unique experiences of every individual. It also involves the promotion of self-determination for each individual. A fourth core value of social work is the importance of human relation- ships. One reason for this is that social workers use human relationships to promote change in individuals, families, groups, and communities. Social workers also understand that helping people to develop healthy human relationships is a means to a high-quality life and happiness for all people. Healthy human relationships are a prerequisite for meeting the needs of love and belonging and for developing healthy families. Integrity is a fifth basic value in social work. Professional social workers must act with integrity at all times. In so doing, social workers develop the trust of clients and coworkers. Social workers also work to promote ethical policies and practices in the organizations in which they are employed. Furthermore, integrity is an important factor for social workers if they are to have the credibility needed to promote social justice. A final core value of the social work profession is competence.Social workers must practice within the areas of their competence and must continually work to develop and enhance their professional expertise. What is more, social workers should look for opportunities to contribute to the profession's knowledge base through education, scientific inquiry, and evaluation of programs and their individual practice.

CODE & ETHICS:
Values relate to what people consider desirable, while "ethics" relates more directly to what people consider right or wrong.27 That is, ethics pertain to values in action. When considering the profession of social work, ethics are important because they relate to expectations associated with professionalconduct. Ethics are so important in social work that the profession has a "code of ethics." This code of ethics spells out social workers' ethical responsibilities to clients, to colleagues, to the social work profession, and to society at large, among other things. They are, in essence, guidelines for professional conduct. Ethics become a challenge for social workers when the professional social worker has a choice between two options, both seemingly ethical, but only one can be chosen. In such a case, which course of action is more ethical and how does one determine this? In other cases, a social worker may have ethical responsibilities to two different parties, say a parent and child, but can only meet his or her responsibility to one party at a time.28 Social workers also confront ethical dilemmas involving confidentiality. They are not supposed to share certain personal information conveyed to them by clients; however, some circumstances may require social workers to do just that in order to protect other people from harm or to protect clients from harming themselves. Examples include suicidal clients and violent spouses. Other ethical dilemmas faced by social workers involve paternalism. Social workers believe in self-determination for clients; however, there are certain circumstances in which social workers may ethically have to direct client behavior in order to keep a client safe. An example would be a mentally ill homeless person who desires to sleep outside during a New England winter instead of using a nearby community shelter. Another illustration would be a social worker who works with children and youth, a population that is not fully mature and therefore does not always exercise mature judgment involving decisions on issues such as sexual relations, alcohol use, and other risk-taking behavior. Social workers in policy and administrative

jobs deal with ethical dilemmas that concern the allocation of scarce resources. How do social workers make ethical choices to fund one program instead of another program? In an environment of scarce resources, social administrators and policymakers must make these decisions frequently. Again, the question is, what is the most ethical option when choosing among several good options? Furthermore, social workers must make ethical decisions involving their professional colleagues. When should a social worker report a colleague who divulges personal client information to others? At what point should a professional social worker report a colleague who makes a sexual comment? When should a social worker report a colleague suspected of drug abuse? Social workers face these and other ethical dilemmas all too frequently. It is the task of professional social work education to assist students in acquiring specific knowledge about social work values and ethics and applying these values and ethics in the field. This includes an awareness of the student's personal values and how they may conflict with the values of the social work profession. It also requires teachers to stimulate awareness of ethical issues on the part of students and help them develop analytical skills to deal with these issues. What is more, by the time students graduate with a social work degree, they should have a sense of moral obligation and personal responsibility concerning the values and ethics of the profession.29 As previously stated, the NASW Code of Ethics provides social work students and professionals with values, principles, and standards to guide their professional conduct. Specifically, the NASW Code of Ethics serves six purposes. First, it identifies the core values of the profession. Second, the code summarizes the broad ethical principles related to social work values and provides ethicalstandards to guide social work practice. Third, the code offers social workers a set of considerations for use in ethical dilemmas. Fourth, it provides ethical standards by which the general public can hold the profession of social work accountable. A fifth purpose, particularly important for students, is that the code helps to socialize practitioners who are new to the field in terms of the profession's mission, values, ethical principles, and ethical standards. And finally, the code of ethics provides the profession with criteria for judging whether or not practicing social workers have been unethical in their conduct.30 More specifically, the aforementioned values and associated ethical principles provided by the NASW Code of Ethics to guide social work practice are quoted as follows:31

Value: Service Ethical Principle: Social workers primary goal is to help people in need and to address social problems. Social workers elevate service to others above self-interest. Social workers draw on their knowledge, values, and skills to help people in need and to address social problems. Social workers are encouraged to volunteer some portion of their professional skills with no expectation of significant financial return (pro bono service).

Value: Social Justice Ethical Principle: Social workers challenge social injustice. Social workers pursue social change, particularly with and on behalf of vulnerable and oppressed individuals and groups of people. Social workers' social change efforts are focused primarily on issues of poverty, unemployment, discrimination, and other forms of social injustice. These activities seek to promote sensitivity to and knowledge about oppression and cultural and ethnic diversity. Social workers strive to ensure access to needed information, services, and resources; equality of opportunity; and meaningful participation in decision making for all people.

Value: Dignity and Worth of the Person Ethical Principle: Social workers respect the inherent dignity and worth of the person. Social workers treat each person in a caring and respectful fashion, mindful of individual differences and cultural and ethnic diversity. Social workers promote clients' socially responsible self-determination. Social workers seek to enhance clients' capacity and opportunity to change and to address their own needs. Social workers are cognizant of their dual responsibility to clients and to the broader society. They seek to resolve conflicts between clients' interests and the broader society's interests in a socially responsible manner consistent with the values, ethical principles, and ethical standards of the profession.

Value: Importance of Human Relationships Ethical Principle: Social workers recognize the central importance of human relationships. Social workers understand that relationships between and among people are an important vehicle for change. Social workers engage people as partners in the helping process. Social workers seek to strengthen relationships among people in a purposeful effort to promote, restore,maintain, and enhance the well-being of individuals, families, social groups, organizations, and communities.

Value: Integrity Ethical Principle: Social workers behave in a trustworthy manner. Social workers are continually aware of the profession's mission, values, ethical principles, and ethical standards and practice in a manner consistent with them. Social workers act honestly and responsibly and promote ethical practices on the part of the organizations with which they are affiliated.

Value: Competence Ethical Principle: Social workers practice within their areas of competence and develop and enhance their professional expertise. Social workers continually strive to increase their professional knowledge and skills and to apply them in practice. Social workers should aspire to contribute to the knowledge base of the profession.

Given these values and ethics, social workers feel that it is important to consistently improve their competence in working with people from various backgrounds and experiences. This involves a special competence in relation to diversity and individual dignity.

The study of how people ought to act in order to be moral. A moral code that guides the conduct of a group of professionals (such as medical doctors).The branch of philosophy that defines what is right for the individual and for society and establishes the nature of obligations, or duties, that people owe themselves and one another. The word ethics is derived from the Greek word ethos, which means "character," and from the Latin word mores, which means "customs." In modern society, it defines how individuals, business professionals, and corporations choose to interact with one another.

Values are the implicit and explicit ideas about what people consider good, ethics relates to what people consider correct or right. Ethics generates standards that direct one's conduct. Social work ethics are behavioral expectations or preferences that are associated with social work responsibility

BY NATIONAL ASSOCIATION OF SOCIAL WORKER'S (NASW).

I.   **The social worker's conduct and comportment as a social worker.**

A.   PROPRIETY:

The social worker should maintain high standards

Of personal conduct in the capacity or identity of social worker.

B.   COMPETENCE AND PROFESSIONAL DEVELOPMENT:

The social worker should strive to become and remain proficient in professional practice and the performance of professional functions.

C.   SERVICE:

The social worker should regard as primary the service obligation of the social work profession.

D. INTEGRITY:

The social worker should act in accordance with the highest standards of professional integrity.

E. SCHOLORSHIP AND RESEARCH:

The social workers engaged in study and research should be guided by the convention of scholarly inquiry.

II.   **The social worker's Ethical responsibilities to clients:**

F. PRIVACY OF CLIENT'S INTERESTS:

The social worker's primary responsibility is

to clients.

G. RIGHTS AND PRE ROGATIVES OF CLIENTS:

The social worker should make
every effort
to foster maximum self-determination on the part of the clients.

H. CONFIDENTILATY AND PRIVACY:

The social worker should respect the privacy of clients and hold in confidence all information obtained in the course of professional service.

I.   FEES:

When setting fees, the social worker should ensure that they are fair, reasonable, considerate, and commensurate with the service performed and with due regard for the client's ability to pay.

III.   **The social worker's Ethical responsibility to colleagues:**

J. RESPECT, FAIRNESS, COURTECY:

The social worker's
should treat
Colleagues with respect, fairness, courtesy, and good faith.

K. DEALING WITH COLLEASUE'S CLIENTS:

The social worker has the responsibility to relate to the client of the colleagues with full professional consideration.

IV.   **The social worker's Ethical responsibility to Employers and Employing organization:**

L. COMMITMENTS TO EMPLOYING ORGANIZATION:

The social worker
should adhere to
Commitments made to the employing organizations.

V.   **The social worker's Ethical responsibility to the social work profession:**

M. MAINTAINING THE INTEGRITY OF THE PROFESSION:

The social worker
should uphold and
Advance the values, ethics, knowledge and mission of the profession.

N. COMMUNITY SERVICE:

The social worker should assist the profession in making social services available to the great public.

O. DEVELOPMENT OF KNOWLEDGE:

The social worker should take responsibility for identifying, developing, and fully utilizing knowledge for professional practice.

VI.   **The social worker's Ethical responsibility to society:**

P. PROMOTING THE GENERAL WELFARE:

The social worker
should promote the general welfare of the society.

VALUES OF SOCIAL WORKER'S

Besides social work profession's commitment during the formation of profession – commitment to quality of life, social justice, human dignity and worth – inclusion of values sets like equality, social justice, freeing of life style, rightful access to social resources and liberation of self-powers are also evident.

Herbert Bisno has classified values/philosophy as followed:

☐ VALUES/PHILOSOPHY RELATING TO INDIVIDUALS:

☐ The social work believes that human

Suffering is undesirable and should be prevented or at least alleviated whenever possible.

☐ Human behavior is the result of interaction

Between the biological organism and its environment.

☐ Family relationship is of primary importance

In the early development of the individual.

☐ Though humans are moral being at birth,

They tend to act irrationally also.

☐ Inherent dignity and worth of human being,

inherent and inalienable right of human being to choose and achieve his own dignity.

☐ VALUES/PHILOSOPHY RELATING TO PROBLEM:

☐ There is serious political, social, and

economic maladjustment in every culture.

☐ Evolutionary type of reform is both possible

and desirable.

☐ Social worker believes in possibility of the

intelligent direction of social change and hence there is a need for social planning.

☐ Appreciating the multi dimensionality of the

problem and its multiple consequences.

☐ VALUES/PHILOSOPHY RELATING TO RELATIONSHIP:

☐ Social work reject the doctrine of laissez

faire and survival of fittest.

☐ The rich and the powerful are not

necessarily "fit", while the poor/weak are not necessarily unfit.

☐ In social work "socialized individuals" are

preferred to "rugged individualism".

☐ A major responsibility for the members

resets with the community.

☐ Accepting the clients / situation as it is and

working at a pace convenient for them.

☐ VALUES/PHILOSOPHY RELATING TO SOCIAL AGENCY:

☐ Social work agencies are basically resources to solve human problems.

☐ VALUES/PHILOSOPHY RELATING TO SOCIAL WORK PRACTICE:

☐ Social work has functionally dualistic

Approach. It attempts to solve individual problems and at the same time simultaneously attempt to modify the social and institutional framework in required direction.

☐ Social work service should be provided by

Professionally trained workers in both public and private agencies.

☐ Social work accepts democracy as the

Fundamental ordering of the society.

☐ Knowledge, skill, ethical standards etc.

Unit – II HISTORICAL DEVELOPMENT
Historical background of social work U.S.A & India – contribution of religious and reform movements for social change and social welfare. Social work – social work education in India – professionalization of social work education.

UNIT – II HISTORICAL DEVELOPMENT
HISTORICAL DEVELOPMENT:
History of social work started from USA and UK in 1200.

1531 – HERRY VIII – identification of beggars.

Beggars were banned in public and give a separate place for them.

Able body homes were formed and people were give jobs.

1601 – Elizabeth.

USA – 1776 war of independence – church – main agency for social services.

1800 – 1900 – Adam smith theory.

1900 onwards – committee – William committee.

Profession of social work started to flourish in Europe with starting of charity organization/association.

1898 – New York school of Philanthropy.

1917 – NY school of social work.

1929 – Economic depression – Federal emergency relief act – need of trained social worker.

1935 – Social security act.(in USA)

1939 – PG first introduced in American school of social work. USA National council on social work education started .

1960 – Anti-poverty – Martin Ruther King USA National council on social work education was started.

IN INDIA:
Started from joint family system in rural areas.

Annie Besant, Raja Ram Mohan Roy given enlightment about social work.

Mumbai – NGO – American Marathi mission.

Clifford Marshal – 1925 – started his work in slums – founder of Nagpada neighborhood house
Approach Tata group 1936 – Sir Doraliji Tata School of social science – 1944 – changed to Tata institution of social science.

1947 – School of social work started in Gujarat and Varanasi.

Gujarat Vidhyapeed, Khesi Vidhyapeed.

1948 – Delhi school of social work.

1950 – Baroda school of social work.

1960 – Madras school of social work.

1962 – Psg school of social work.

1970 – Madurai school of social work.

1980 – Bishop college Trichi. Screed hearts college in Tirupatur

CONTRIBUTION OF RELIGIOUS REFORM MOVEMENTS IN INDIA
Though social work is not practiced in its present form, serving the people and helping the needy has been considered almost a moral duty to everyone. In this regard several prescriptions are also laid down for the individuals to follow. Traditionally social work in India is more person based and not institution based. Religion philosophical foundation of social work in India is better understood to the following three major titles. 1. Social welfare during Vedic Period 2. Hinduism and the philosophy of social welfare. 3. Buddhism and the philosophy of social welfare. 4. Jainism and the philosophy of Social Welfare

1. **Social welfare** during Vedic Period the Vedas are the scriptures derived from the Vedic period (c. 1500-700 BC)

Communitarian (a social order in which individuals are bound together by common values that foster close communal bonds. A model of political organization that stresses ties of affection, kinship, and a sense of common purpose and tradition, as opposed to the meager morality of contractual ties entered into between a loose conglomeration of individuals) republics existed during the early Vedic period. In communitarian social order the whole business of helping people in need was everybody's business mainly handles in a collective way. Thus everybody was client and agent both a different occasions and for different purposes. In early days of Indian civilization both social life and social welfare were almost inseparable

2. **Hinduism** and the philosophy of social welfare. According to Hindu philosophy human beings

should revere, respect and love all, because, God, the supreme being pervades all and immanent in all things and beings. The goal of life is to realize the self, which is nothing but GOD, for this one needs to rise into higher spheres of thinking, feeling and acting and help others to achieve the same. The rules and regulation prescribed to achieve self-realization are known as Manushya Dharmas. It iselaborated as yamas (actions to be avoided) and niyamas (actions to be followed) these virtues are enriched by the additional virtues of Dana, Daya and Kshanthi Dana: it is understood as charity in the form of alms giving to the deserving. Daya means compassion to all Kshanthi patience and forgiveness. The popular Hindu saying expresses Janata Seva is Janardana Seva. The service of man is the service of God. Janata Seva means helping the people. Serving his fellow human beings is an instrument to realize self – God or Janardana. The reward for Janata Seva is the enlargement of the self.

At later days, Mary Richmond, a social work pioneer, while explaining the underlying philosophy of social work, mentioned about wider self. The concept of wider self-match the Hindu concept of larger or greater self.

3. **Buddhism** and the philosophy of social welfare. By the performance of acts of punna (punyam) and the avoidance of acts (pavam) of papa one contributes to social welfare while gradually transforming oneself in such a way that noble qualities of mind conducive to produce the maturity and insight that bring full liberation of the mind could sooner or later be attained. Until such time as one attains the final liberation, acts of punna protect a person from falling into unhappy rebirths and furnishes one with all the desirable material conditions of living. Buddhism provides a great incentive to believers by emphasizing the effects of punna_deeds to engage in acts of social welfare. The concept of punna is connected with the doctrines of kamma and rebirth. These doctrines appeal to the concern of everyone with one's own interest and have the effect of preventing people who have faith in them to avoid engaging in any conduct that is productive of suffering to others and encouraging them to do positive good to others which is productive of beneficial effects to themselves.

It is to be noted that the Buddhist notion of social welfare is wider than a purely mundane notion in such a way that it includes an awareness of the material needs that are necessary for the promotion of social welfare. The welfare of people can be promoted only when all their needs are adequately fulfilled. Humanist psychologists have pointed out that human beings have a hierarchy of needs. Xv They do not attain their real humanity unless certain higher and uniquely human needs are also satisfied. Buddhism can fully agree with that view, for Buddhism recognizes the necessity to attend to the basic material needs of man not as an end in itself, but as a means to an end which is much higher than that. The greatest happiness that a human being can attain by becoming entirely free from the corruptions of mind is considered in Buddhism as the highest in the hierarchy of human needs.

4. **Jainism** and the philosophy of social welfare. Jains believe that all living beings possess a soul, and therefore great care and awareness is required in going about one's business in the world. Jainism is a religion in which all life is considered worthy of respect and it emphasizes this equality of all life, advocating the protection of even the smallest creatures. This goes as far as the life of a fly. A major characteristic of Jain belief is the emphasis on the consequences of not only physical but also mental behaviors.

5. **Islam** is the name of a religion founded by Muhammad in ancient Arabia in the 7th century. People who follow Islam are called Muslims. They believe in only one God, That God is called Allah, which is the Arabic phrase for "the (only) God". Islam has more followers than Roman Catholicism with 1.3 billion followers which makes it the world's largest religion dating today. It is also the fastest growing religion in the world.

The Five Pillars of Islam There are five things that Muslims should do. They are called "The Five Pillars of Islam". 1. Faith: The Testimony (al-Shaada in Arabic) is the Muslim belief that there is no god but Allah Himself, and that Muhammad is His messenger. 2. Prayer: Muslims pray five times at special times of the day. 3. Charity: Muslims who have money must give alms (Zakah or Zakat in Arabic) to help poor Muslims in the local community. 4. Fasting: Muslims fast during Ramadan, They do not eat or drink from sunrise till sunset for one lunar month. 5. Hajj (Pilgrimage): Muslims in general who can afford or who have made the Hajj must buy an animal according to the Islamic criteria to sacrifice and cook as food or give away to the poor, if they have the money for it.

6. Christianity Christianity is a faith based on the believed life and teaching of Jesus. Christians

believe by faith that all who sin (disobey God) even once wouldn't go to heaven, even if they did good things, so God gave His own Son, Jesus, to die, so that Christians can "substitute" Jesus' sinless life for themselves. Christians believe that no matter how many sins or how much evil a person has done, they will still go to heaven by taking Jesus as a substitute for his/her own sin. It is a unique religion in the sense that the believer's good or bad deeds do not determine their eternal salvation. Rather, it is the sinless life of Jesus and the sacrificial death of Jesus that is the way to heaven. Thus, Jesus is their "Savior" and they are "saved" by Him, and not because of anything they did on their own.

Charity -Showing love for people the word "Charity" gets its roots form the Latin word "caritas", meaning love. In 1 Peter 4:8a (King James Version), Peter writes; "And above all things have fervent "charity" among yourselves." Simply put, this verse says that a Christian is to have complete love to each other. And in Mark 12:31b (King James Version) Jesus, when asked what was the greatest commandment, replied that first is to love the Lord, "And the second is like, namely this, Thou shalt "love" thy neighbor as thyself. There is none other commandment greater than these." So in Jesus' own words, it is vital to the Christian belief, that a Christian, have Charity (or love), to each other.

Contributions of Ancient Indian Kings to Social Welfare

Ashoka, the Great As the third emperor of the Mauryan dynasty, Ashoka was born in the year 304 B.C. His greatest achievements were spreading Buddhism throughout his empire and beyond. He set up an ideal government for his people and conquered many lands, expanding his kingdom. H. G. Wells wrote of Ashoka: In the history of the world there have been thousands of kings and emperors who called themselves 'their highnesses,' 'their majesties,' and 'their exalted majesties' and so on. They shone for a brief moment, and as quickly disappeared. But Ashoka shines and shines brightly like a bright star, even unto this day.

Kanishka Kanishka was a king of the Kushan Empire in Central Asia, ruling an empire extending to large parts of India in the 2nd century of the Common Era, famous for his military, political, and spiritual achievements. His main capital was at Peshawar (Purushpura) in northwestern Pakistan, with regional capitals at the location of the modern city of Taxila in Pakistan, Begram in Afghanistan and Mathura in India.

GuptaChandra Gupta Ghatotkacha (c. 280–319) AD, had a son named Chandra Gupta. In a breakthrough deal, Chandra Gupta was married to a Lichchhavi—the main power in Magadha. With a dowry of the kingdom of Magadha (capital Pataliputra) i, conquering much of maghadas, Prayaga and Saketa. He established a realm stretching from the Ganga River (Ganges River) to Prayaga (modern-day Allahabad) by 321.

Sultanate   The Delhi Sultanate refers to the many Muslim dynasties that ruled in India from 1206 to 1526. Several Turkic and Pashtun ("Afghan") dynasties ruled from Delhi: the Mamluk dynasty (1206-90), the Khilji dynasty (1290-1320), the Tughlaq dynasty (1320-1413), the Sayyid dynasty (1414-51), and the Lodhi dynasty (1451-1526). In 1526 the Delhi Sultanate was absorbed by the emerging Mughal Empire.

Deccan sultanates The Deccan sultanates were five Muslim-ruled late medieval kingdoms-- Bijapur, Golkonda, Ahmadnagar, Bidar, and Berar of south- central India. The Deccan sultanates were located on the Deccan Plateau, between the Krishna River and the Vindhya Range. These kingdoms became independent during the breakup of the Bahmani Sultanate. In 1490, Ahmadnagar declared independence, followed by Bijapur and Berar in the same year. Golkonda became independent in 1518 and Bidar in 1528. In 1510, Bijapur repulsed an invasion by the Portuguese against the city of Goa, but lost it later that year.

Mughal Rule India in the 16th century had numerous unpopular rulers, both Muslim and Hindu, with an absence of common bodies of laws or institutions. External developments also played a role in the rise of the Mughal Empire. The circumnavigation of Africa by the Portuguese explorer Vasco da Gama in 1498 allowed Europeans to challenge Arab control of the trading routes between Europe and Asia. In Central Asia and Afghanistan, shifts in power pushed Babur of Ferghana (in present-day Uzbekistan) southward, first to Kabul and then to India. The Mughal Empire lasted for more than three centuries. The Mughal Empire was one of the largest centralized states in pre modern history and was the precursor to the British Indian Empire.

Professionalization of social work education

Professional training in social work in India was initiated by Dr. Clifford Manshardt, an American protestant missionary. He came to India in 1925 through the American Marathi mission, a Protestant Christian organization. This organization worked in slum communities of Bombay and founded the Nagapada Neighborhood House in 1926, headed by Dr.Clifford Manshardt as its first Director. The agency was similar to Settlement House in its objective and activities. It was located in an area, which had many social problems including poverty, gambling and prostitution. Such problems were the result of the fast changing social structure, which had weakened the family bond and community togetherness. Manshardt mooted the idea of developing a school of social work to meet the need for trained manpower to work in Indian conditions. With financing from the Sir Dorabji Tata Trust, the first school founded in 1936 was known as Sir Dorabji Graduate School of Social Work later renamed as Tata Institute of Social Sciences in 1944.

Since then, Social work education in India has spawned seven decades during which it has attracted a large number of youth to pursue a formal degree in Social Work, develop human service values and work for the betterment of society. The journey has not been without its fair share of bumps and jerks, but challenging and exciting, nevertheless. The problems these trained social workers confront are common in Indian subcontinent. In order to ensure excellence in education, training and practice of professional social work, we need very active professional associations. Though India has fairly a long history of social work education as compared to other South Asian countries, professional associations were formed much later in order to play huge proactive roles. Our existing associations are yet to get permanent affiliation or membership in International Federation of Social Workers (IFSW). As professionals we have a responsibility for making professional organizations vibrant. In past, we had several associations such as

Labor Welfare Officers" Association, Probation Officers" Association, Association of Alumni of Schools of Social Work in India, etc. There are few regional level associations as well, such as, Bombay Association of Trained Social Workers (BATSW), Maharashtra Association of Social Work Educators (MATSWE), Karnataka Association of Professional Social Workers (KAPSW), Professional Social Workers Forum, Chennai (PSWFC), etc. The ambit of their activities rarely reaches beyond local level meetings, seminars and they do not have much say or authority at the national level. The professional bodies of social workers that function at the national level are mainly three, namely, ASSWI, ISPSW and NAPSWI. Associations of Schools of Social Work in India (ASSWI) ASSWI was established in 1959 at Baroda. It is a professional organization engaged in the promotion of standards of social work education in the country. It has represented the profession by taking up social issues and concerns related to social work education at the national level since the early sixties. This association is functioning through its elected executive committee. Most of the members of ASSWI are from Schools of Social Work/Departments of Social Work which were established during the second half of the 20th century.

The Indian Society of Professional Social Work (ISPSW) The Indian Society of Professional Social Work (ISPSW) is the oldest association of professional social workers in India. It has been geared towards the goal of Empowering Society for Social Development. The Society was formerly known as Indian Society of Psychiatric Social Work. It was established in the year 1970 by Dr. R.K.Upadhyaya and his staff of the Dept. of Psychiatric Social Work, Central Institute of Psychiatry, Ranchi. The present name of the Society was considered in the year 1988, because of an increased representation of the trainers, practitioners and researchers of all specialization of Social Work. The association primarily focuses on uniting the professional social workers to debate, discuss and develop conceptual frameworks and feasible indigenous interventions of social work for practice in India. In order to facilitate this purpose, the Society has conducted many annual Conferences seminars and symposia on various social issues, all over India. Many of the life members of this Society are representing various reputed National and International organizations, Universities and other agencies all over the World. The Society regularly identifies and felicitates esteemed personalities from the Social Work and its related fields.

National Association of Professional Social Workers in India (NAPSWI) NAPSWI is a non profit, non- political, national level organization dedicated to the promotion of standard and status of social work profession in India. The association received legal status as a society under the Society Registration Act XXI of 1860 on 9th September 2005. This national association comprises social work institutions, schools and departments, educators, practitioners as well as students from every state in the country. Senior citizens are also provided membership. NAPSWI intends to fulfill the twin purpose of promoting the social work profession across the country with the aim of improving the quality of services in the social welfare and social development sectors on one hand and to protect interests of social work professionals on the other hand. NAPSWI aims to advance excellence in education, training and practice of professional social work through - Education, Research, Training, Networking, Advocacy and Resource Development. Objectives of NAPSWI are as follows:

□ Increase awareness about social work profession at various levels; □ Promote the highest professional standards and ethics in the practice of professional social work; □ Advance the knowledge and practice base of social work interventions that enhance quality of life and standard of living of persons, their family and environment; □ Faster communication and support among professional social workers;

Promote social change, empowerment and liberation of people to enhance their well being adhering to the principles of human rights and social justice; Promote research, action and other forms of continuing education for knowledge up- gradation of members; and Advocate for programs and policies to meet the needs of social work fraternity and its various clientele groups. With the launching of social work program by dint of Open and Distance Learning in India through IGNOU, a new chapter has been opened for professional social workers in the Indian sub-continent since 2004.This initiative of IGNOU has taken social work education to the door steps of the un- reached in far flung areas i.e. from Kashmir to Campbell Bay in Andaman and Nicobar Islands and all the states in the North-East. There is flexible admission procedures adopted by IGNOU: anyone having the required entry qualification can pursue social work education at Bachelors, Masters and Doctoral level without restrictions on age, place of residence and occupational status. The Annual National Seminar being organized by IGNOU in collaboration with NAPSWI is a meeting place for professional social work educators, practitioners and students from any state and union territory in the country. This annual event is gaining momentum with the support of ASSWI, several universities and international organizations.

Unit – III METHODS OF SOCIAL WORK
A brief understanding of methods of social work – social case work – social group work – community organization – social work research – social action – social welfare administration.

Social Work methods are purely professional knowledge, not barrowed from any other disciplines. It is also called social work practice. These methods and application differentiate social work and many others social sciences that base mere on theoretical knowledge. For instance, sociology, psychology, anthropology and philosophy all lack specific methods like social work although having well advanced theory.

1. **Primary method:** are that systematic and planned way of performing an activity, which is fundamental to Social Work. These are just like roots of social work, which give birth to other branches.

2. **Secondary method:** these are secondary because it facilitates the primary methods. There are also the derivatives of primary methods.
   Primary method:

1. **Social Case Work**

2. **Social Group Work**

3. **Social Organization and development**
   Secondary method:

1. **Social Research**

2. **Social Action**

3. **Social Welfare Administration**
   Social Case Work:
   Social Case Work, a primary method of social work, is concerned with the adjustment and

development of individual towards more satisfying human relations. Better family life, improved schools, better housing, more hospitals and medical care facilities, protected economic conditions and better relations between religious groups help the individual in his adjustment and development. But his adjustment and development depend on the use of these resources by him. Sometimes due to certain factors, internal or external, he fails to avail existing facilities. In such situations, social caseworker helps him. Thus, social casework is one to one relationship, which works in helping the individual for his adjustment and development.

Every individual reacts differently to his social, economic and physical environments and as such problems of one individual are different from those of another. The practice of casework is a humanistic attempt for helping people who have difficulty in coping with the problems of daily living. It is one of the direct methods of social work which uses the case-by-case approach for dealing with individuals or families as regards their problems of social functioning. Case work, aims at individualized services in the field of social work in order to help the client to adjust with the environments.

Origin of Case work by working with the poor Social Workers radically realized that forces within the individual and forces external to him contributed for human suffering. Though casework as a mode of helping people on the basis of a person-to-person relationship was present in every society from ancient times, the professional method of casework originated in U.S.A. in the second decade of this century. One of the earliest organised efforts in U.S.A. to help the poor was the establishment of the American Charity Organization Society (1) in 1877 on the pattern of the Charity Organization of London, which was started seven years earlier. One of the aims of the society was to find out ways and means of helping the poor and needy and thus to organise individualised services geared to this purpose. The society used volunteers, who were called friendly visitors, to visit the homes of the poor for purposes of assessing their need, for rendering material assistance and for giving them guidance and advice. The friendly visitors were subsequently supplemented by 'paid agents'. These paid helpers gradually developed, systematic procedures in performing their tasks. They collected data about the needy individuals and families, and helped them after assessing their need. They also maintained records in which they kept all the information including personal data, as well as the type of help rendered. It was out of the practice of these early workers that caseworkdeveloped gradually to a professional method in subsequent years. Their collective experience of knowing the poor families and their problems and the concurrent studies of poverty by social scientists broadened the understanding of human behaviour. There was the growing recognition that there were forces within the individual and forces external to him which influenced his behaviour and the nature of his existence in society. In course of time the terms 'paid agents' and 'the poor' were supplanted by caseworkers and clients respectively in the terminology of the help giving organisation and the office of the organisation came to be known as the agency.

Definitions of Social Case Work

Mary Richmond (1915) "Social Case Work may be defined as the Art of doing different things with different people, co-operating with them to achieve some of their own & society"s betterment."

Jarrett (1919) Social case work is "the art of bringing an individual who is in a condition of social disorder into the best possible relation with all parts of his environment".

Taft (1920) Social case work means "social treatment of a maladjusted individual involving an attempt to understand his personality, behaviour and social relationships and to assist him in working out better social and personal adjustment".

Lee (1923) Social case work is the art of changing human attitudes"

Hollis (1954) "Social Case work is a method employed by social worker to help individuals find solution to problems of social adjustment which they are unable to handle in satisfactory way by their own efforts."

Objectives of Social Case Work

1. To make good rapport with the common people.
2. To find-out, understand & solve the internal problems of an individual.
3. To strengthen ones ego power.
4. To prevent problem.
5. To develop internal resources.

Nature & Characteristics of Case Work

1. Relationship arise out of shared & emotionally charged situation.
2. Relationship contains elements of acceptance, expectation, support & stimulation.
3. Client & case worker are interdependent.
4. Case work relationship may have several therapeutic values.
5. Improvement of condition.
6. More adjustment within the society.
7. Development of personality.
8. Capacity building.
9. Relationship needs outside help.
10. Case worker too has relationship reactions and part of and part of one's professional skills in their management.

BASIC COMPONENTS OF CASE WORK:

- Person
- Problem
- Place
- Process

PRINCIPLES OF CASE WORK:

- Principles of individualization.
- Principles of powerful expression of feeling.
- Principles of controlled emotional involvement.
- Principles of acceptance.
- Principles of non-judgmental attitude.
- Principles of confidentiality.
- Principles of determination.
- Principles of developing and utilizing resource.

SOCIAL GROUP WORK

Human being is a social animal; they can't live without the social interaction, and community life. Social interaction is one of the indirect ways learning by doing. A child learns with in his own group and also takes knowledge from the groups that are child focused or any others. The social groups working for the children play important role in individual child life. Group first assesses the ability and weakness of a child and then relates him /her accordingly to other groups within the child reach in a school, community or an institution. The establishment of satisfying group life outside the family is pre- requisite for effective social living, which every individual must accomplish though out his life. To some children it comes naturally for others it may have to be developed and foster. So group addresses those who need care for the development of social habit that further help them in social development. Mutual give and take policy enables the members of the child group and assistance from the outside group to evolved mutually satisfying social relationship among themselves. An early childhood good experience being with family or assisted by the groups developed positive attitude of the children that goes along with his/her life. So group intervention aim is to give a constructive and satisfying group experience to children and individuals. The children are likely to adopt constructive and good behaviors and approaches also   in   other   sphere   of   life. Social casework is not the whole of social work. All human beings do not live alone. They grow up in families, tribes; communities' etc. group life is basic for every human being. Another important area of social work is social group work, which deals with the individuals as a member of the group. Some definitions of social group work are:

1. Social group work is that method of social work, which helps individuals in the improvement of their social functioning and the achievement of desirable social goals.

2. Social group work is the method which helps the individuals to enhance the social functioning through purposeful group experience and cope more effectively with their problems.

3. According to H. B. Trecker, group work is "A process and a method through which individual groups in social agency setting are helped by a worker to relate themselves to other people and to experience growth opportunities in accordance with their needs and capacities".

Social group worker does not concentrate on individual alone. It helps in educational development and cultural growth of the members of the groups. The worker is interested in helping the individuals through guided group interaction.

Principles of Social Group Work:

The group worker must understand the basic principles of social group work and must be guided by them in his professional practice. Principles are guiding statements that have come from experience or research. Their generalizations are based upon what has been observed good practice with groups in different situations.
The purpose of these principles is to guide the group worker who needs knowledge of the individuals and groups' behavior and social conditions as well as the ability to work efficiently with the group of people.
H. B Trecker in his masterpiece "Social Group Work – Principles and Practice", has given the following principles of social group work:

Principle of planned group formation: The group is the basic unit through which individuals are helped to grow physically, socially, culturally and psychologically. The first task of the group worker is to form a group. The group workers should be aware about the needs and resources of the group and also their potentialities limitations and the cultural values of the areas.

Principle of helping or enabling function: The function of the group worker is helping or enabling function. So, he should solve his problems on self-help basis. The objective should be according to the wishes and capabilities and help them for the solution of their problems within their own resources through self-help basis.

Principle of purposeful relationship: Group work method requires the worker to form purposeful relationship with group members, which means that they should focus on the needs of the people, which are expressed by the members. We can achieve such relationship through self-knowledge and self-disciplined.

Principle of organization: The organization of the group should be flexible, should be adjustable in various situations. It should change with the needs of the group and according to the change situations for the smooth function of the group.

Principle of self-decision or planning: The group must be helped to make its own decision, its own planning and programmes and the members should take the responsibility according to their ability.

Principle of programme acceptance: the members of the group according to their capabilities, educational level, needs, experience and socio-economic level should accept Programme of the group. These programmes should progress in relation to the developing capacity of the group.

Principle of people: Without acceptance this programme by the people it cannot give the good results. The social group worker should convince the people to accept this programme, which is aimed at the solution of their felt needs. They people should accept the advice to solve their mutual respect and love increases the good relationships, which helps in understanding of social group worker and group and for the solution of the problems and for the development of the programmer.

Principle of best utilization of resources: The group and community resources should be utilized in relation to the group and individual needs for the benefits of the group as a whole.

Principle of individualization: The individual should be convinced in a way that he should feel to contribute to the group welfare. However the individual and the group should feel for the development and new changes in the community.

Principle of evaluation: The continuous evaluation of the group work process and the progress is essential. The group worker should evaluate the progress in accordance with the prescribed standard. In Pakistan, social group work method is used in community centers, hospitals, and educational and other institutions. The principles of social group work can successfully apply not only in the limited fields but also in the larger fields of social welfare and even in working with other political, social and religious group.

Social group in the ordinary sense means that any collection of more than one individual, but sociologically it is a collection of individuals interacting with each other under a recognized structure. A social group is always motivated by some common goals and interests, characterized by some rules and regulations (formal and informal), which regulates the behavior of its members.

Ogburn defines it: The group in a statement "We feelings". We feelings mean that the members of the group develop basic responses for each other. The following are some of the essential characteristics, which distinguish a group from a non-group:

1. Collection of individuals

2. Psychological interaction.

3. Common goals and interaction.

4. Group norms.

Types of group:

There are two types of groups:

1.   Primary and   2. Secondary

1.   Primary Group:

It is a small group in which a small number of persons come in to direct contact with one another. They meet face to face for mutual help, companionship and discussion of common questions. They live in the presence and thought of one another. The characteristics can be achieved in the following ways:

1. Face to face interaction among the members.

2. Mutual aid among themselves

3. Realization of common problems among the group members.

The primary group is the primary in the sense that the members within the group are emotionally, attitudes, ideas and habits of individual develop with this group and these things depend upon:

1. Frequency of interaction among themselves.

2. The duration of interaction among the members.

3. Intensity of social context.

4. Common object of interaction among the members.

Characteristics   of   Primary   Group:

Intimate feelings and close relationship. In a primary group, we directly cooperate with our fellows and our relations with them are more personal. A group may be called primary because it has exerted an influence in the early life of a man that is before other groups could influence him. Family in this sense is a primary group because its influence over the child at the earliest. In a primary group, men do the same thing together with the cooperation of each other. Their relations are face to face to achieve their common interest. All the members participate in this process and they share common experience and have a common aim. These may be a division of Labour in primary groups. Thus in a primary group:

1. There is physical closeness among members.

2. The members have common aims.

3. The relations of the members are an end in them.

4. The relations of the members are spontaneous.

5. Members have personal relations.

6. There is continuity in the relations of the members.

Secondary Group:

Secondary group is one, which is large in size; city, political party and labor union etc. Here the human contacts are undefined and superficial. They have direct influence over the others. They know personally only few members and their function. Here cooperation with his fellow work is indirect. According to Paul Landis "Secondary groups are those that are relatively casual and impersonal in their relationship. Relationship in them is usually complicated rather than mutually helpful".

Difference between Primary and Secondary group:

The following are the main points of difference between primary and secondary group:

Size: Primary group is small in size as well as in area. The membership is limited to small number and usually confined to a defined area. It is not spread over the wide world. In a secondary group, the membership and area is large. The membership is scattered in different parts of the world.

Types of structure: Every secondary group is regulated on formal rules. A formal authority is set up with designated powers and clear-cut division of labor in which function of each other is specified in relation to the function of all the rest fellows. Primary group is based on informal structure. The members participate in the same process. There is spontaneous adjustment in the working of the group. There is no formal and detail. The structure is simple in the primary group.

Kind of co-operation: In a primary group, the members directly cooperate with each other, participating in the same process. They sit together, discuss together, play together and decide together. In a secondary group, the cooperation with the fellow members is indirect. The members cooperate only to achieve the group's objectives. It is not the process that binds them together but the object to whose attainment, they unite. They do not work together but one work for the other.

Relationship: In the primary group, the relationships of the members are direct and personal. They meet face to face and develop direct contacts. In the secondary group, the relationships are not direct and personal because they do not live in same place and thought of one another. They just work with each other and see each other.

Community organization

Social work in community setting is to organize, mobilize and help the communities to identify their own needs with resources in the community to address those needs accurately, and motivate community members to realize their aspirations. The social worker role is empathetic, to felt himself as a community member and realize on the same way as each member of the community feel the problem. Then he tries to teach the community with skill and knowledge of community development. This makes the community empowered to help themselves and become self-reliant. Sympathetic approach on other hand on the part of the social worker will leads to dependency. As in sympathy the helper mostly extend all sort of help without the community involvement. Each community having problem is also full of resources. No one can resolve the community problem and to address it as accurately as the community can do. There is a common proverb, "That the village rabbit can be caught easily by the village dog", as the dog of the village better knows the ways to her home, her eating, playing timing. Social worker just enables the community to work in an organized way.

Concept and Approaches of community work- Directive and non-directive approaches

A community is broadly defined as any group of people, within a specified physical, geographical boundary, that comes together for a common purpose or goal. A community can be a rural village, a displacement camp, and a group of children living on the street together or a neighborhood in an urban city. In communities, the leaders of the community can include: traditional leaders, religious leaders, elders, clan chief, women leaders, youth leaders and traditional healers and others. The people can elect the leaders or self-selected due to force or for a specific role or job. These leaders are usually responsible for maintaining law and order and for resolving the problems of their people. Importantly, leaders along with parents are the Duty Bearers of the community's children and have the responsibility for their care and protection Concept of participation, empowerment, leadership, power dynamics, conflict and its management, social mobilization, and gender/ non-discrimination issues in community and other types [of discrimination]

DEFINITION
Community development is the process of planning and developing social services in order to meet the health and welfare needs of a community.
Richard W. Pastern defines it as:
"An organized body of knowledge which deals comprehensively with the community and with all of the various functions of the community life as integrated parts of the whole."
Gangrade, K. D. 1971 defined community organisation as a:
"The process by which the efforts of people themselves are united with government authorities to improve the economic, social and cultural conditions of communities to integrate these communities into the life of nation and to enable them to contribute fully to national progress."

Principles of community organization:

- Acceptance of community: The community organizer should accept the community and should act in a way that the community should accept him and if he has some problem, he should study that and contact the local leaders in this regards and then approach the community to the interest for the welfare of people in the community.

- Understanding of felt needs and resources: The community worker should know the felt needs of the people and their resources and they should start work according to those felt needs. They should also explore available resources, which are available outside the community.

- Individualization: Community worker should always try to identify problems faced by some individuals and group and should repair special plans and programmers for them to make them participate with other groups or individual of the community. By this we mean that individual's attention is also necessary for the community workers.

- Self-determination: Community worker should provide full freedom to the local community to determine their needs and problems and resources act their own and should also give plans for their solution. He should encourage them in the planning for solution of these problems and should not impose his own views on them.

- Freedom within limits: The social worker should guide the community and make them free in giving the ideas of all about the solution of the problems but in decisions should not close the limits to violate the interest of the group but the decision should be in the common interest of the community.

- Empathy, not sympathy: Community worker's attitude as also his approach towards work with the community should be non-judgmental. Whenever any decision is to be taken, it should be based on objective facts concerning community life and values cherished by the community, not by the worker.

- Flexibility: The community worker should involve various members of the community in different matters and also delicate authority to them. The community workers should also be flexible to give rise to new leadership according to change situation.

- Progress programme experience: All the programmes in the community should be evolutionary and not revolutionary. All the programmes chalked out by the community and should take in to consideration the local needs and problems with the involvement of people in the community.

☐   People's participation: The community worker should involve in the identification of all issues, problems, needs and resources and also development plans for this area. This participation should be from the first stage till final decision is taken.

☐   Good or meaningful relationship: The community worker should establish good relationship in the community. He should need all the groups and sub-groups of the community and should understand their problems. This would enable him to involve the community as long as he feels. They had developed capacity to lead as he deals at with their own felt needs and problems.

☐   Mobilization: The community organizer should mobilize its all resources whether internal or external to avoid duplication of efforts. He should utilize these resources. He should also explore the talents and ability of different groups in the community. It is very necessary for the development of community.

☐   Evaluation: The community worker should evaluate his work and people participation. He should also find out the various drawbacks and the groups between the various programmes of the community development. The purpose of the evaluation is to readjust you according to the change situation.

SOCIAL RESEARCH
Definitions:
According to P. K Young:
"Social research is the systematic method of discovering new facts, their sequence; inter relationships, casual explanations and social laws which govern them."
According to Webster:
"A studious enquiry usually critical and exhaustive investigation or experimentation having for its aim the revision of accepted conclusions in the light of newly accepted facts."
According to CORDESCO:
"Research is systematic search for relevant information in a specific topic".
According to LUNDBERG:
"A method sufficiently objective and systematic to make possible classification, generalization and verification of the data observed."
Importance of Social work Research:

In the social research, we collect empirical data of facts through research. It is an organized effort to acquire new knowledge about various aspects of society and social issues. Its scope includes various methods of treatment, rehabilitation, identification of social needs and problems and knowledge about community resources.
Social planning would be ineffective without proper research, which enables the planners to access the needs of the community. It also helps them to refine social work techniques and methods used for solving social problems.
For the development of an area or even for personality development, it is necessary to get information and then on the basis of this information's, we plan for the future. Social work is a problem solving method, so before getting into process to its solution, we must obtain important information regarding the issue that when, where, why, and how the problem started and to solve it. All these information can be collected through a process, which is called social work research.

☐   It increases our knowledge about various issues especially on the basis   on which we are doing social research.

☐   Their conclusions based on research are more authentic or reliable.

☐   It can be applied in all fields of human life because every field of human life needs some facts to meet every day problem and research provides factual data.

- Research gives us clear picture of a social problem because in order to solve any social problem, we need to have a clear picture of the e.g. what is the nature of the problem, how it emerges, how it is effecting the people, how many people have being influenced and how can we solve it.

- Research is important for planning and evaluating certain programmes e.g. if you want to start social welfare programmes, you must collect relevant data from the people in order to find out their views about this programme. And if the attitude of the people towards this programme is positive then it should be introduced.

- Social research enables social worker to make their programme more effective, useful and should help them to refine social work techniques and methods used for solving social problems.

- Social research develops and discovers new facts and also verifies the old facts.

- Research is helpful in the public relations programmes because in public relations, we know their problems, requirements, needs, priorities and their tastes.

- Through research, we can evaluate our programmes and know the cause of its success and failure.

- Through social research, we help the administration for streaming their priorities, (in the light of information's we get through research) liking fixing of pay scale, cost of living, allowances and priorities of the locality etc.

- Research Process

   Like other social sciences, certain steps are required in the field of social work research too for conducting research on scientific lines. These steps are as follows:
   Selection of subject: On the basis of experience and available information, the research formulates the problem under study. It may be either a specific aspect or includes the total aspects of the problem. The problem selected should be relevant to the branch of social work where the researcher is going to study.
   Formulation of hypothesis: After selecting the problem, the researcher gathers certain ideas about the problem. This process is known as hypothesis. According to George Lundberg: "The hypothesis is tentative justification the validity of which remains to be tested." In its most elementary stage the hypothesis may be guess, imaginative ideas that becomes the basis for investigation.
   Construction of a research design: For social work research, it is necessary to prepare a research design. The research design enables the worker to carry on his work systematically. The research should be formulated carefully and once the design has been prepared, it is easy to test the hypothesis, analyze data and take other steps.
   Survey of literature related to the problem: Mere selection of problem is not sufficient. For proper understanding of the problem the worker has to survey the literature related to that problem.
   Investigation and study of material related to the problem: No study is completed in self. There are various matters and topics related to the problem. For proper study it is necessary to investigate and study the material related to the problem. This investigation and study is helpful in taking the future steps.
   Collection of data: After preparing the research design, the process of data collection is started. For this purpose, first step is the collection of data or facts pertaining to the problem.
   Tabulation of collected data: Mere collection of data is not sufficient for research. For proper study of the problem, it is necessary that data should be systematically

tabulated and classified. This step helps the worker to proceed in the right direction.

Analysis and interpretation of data: Once data has been tabulated and classified, the worker proceeds to analyze and interpret it. On the basis of tabulation, the worker is able to categorize the data according to its characteristics. This makes the analysis and interpretation of data easy.

Verification of the problem and hypothesis: After analysis and interpretation of data, the researcher verifies the problem and the hypothesis. Without verification, it is not possible to arrive at any correct result.

Generalization: Once hypothesis has been proved to be correct as a result of verification, certain general principles can be laid down. These general principles are based on the results of the analysis and verification of the data scientifically tabulated and classified.

Types of social research:

Pure Research: To know or understand for the satisfaction of knowing or understanding the facts of our environment, their relationships or their implications without any application in view is called Pure Research. Pure Research is designed without reference to practical research. Pure research helps us in developing general principles and theoretical knowledge offers solutions to many practical problems.

Applied or action research: Applied research is action oriented and social workers are concerned with them. Science is a problem solving process. The science, which is capable of solving problem, is called Applied Research. In applied research, we design certain studies and then find out certain facts. It aims at developmental work i.e. the utilization of the intellectual knowledge towards economic or social ends.

Tools of research

Schedule

Questionnaire

Interview and visits

Records

Preparation of report

Survey:

Survey is mostly conducted to collect the facts from the field about an issue or a problem. Before survey a sample has been taken from the population as no one can reach every individual. Stakeholders in the communities are identified for interview. Special questioners are design to conduct different survey. Those are filled from the individuals and groups. The data collected during the survey is compiled for the final report.

Survey has many good characteristics. It gives in depth knowledge of the issue and problems. It is mostly conducted with consultation of the community people who are more aware of the issue as compared to the out- sider. The finding of the survey is based for future planning of any project. The project success and failure are also depending on the accuracy of the survey. If the real stakeholders were contacted and the questioner was designed according to the needs of the project, the data will be more accurate and useful. Other wise the result will be opposite

Interviews:

Interview are very useful for gaining information on the perceptions and beliefs of people; their ideas for change and their opinions on what motivates, demotivates, frustrates, and encourages them; and the organizational norms and culture. However, there are strong potentials for bias in the hands of those who are untrained, careless, or very normative, and not all interview information may be accurate.

Interviews are one of the most valuable sources of information about an individual, family, community and an organization; their usefulness far exceeds their cost in most cases. However, the quality of the interviewer and data coder is essential to the accuracy of the information.

Types of Interviews

Interviews let you tap into a wealth of ideas, while immersing yourself in the organizational culture. They can bring up many thoughts and perspectives, which surveys miss, and can completely turn around the interviewer's ideas about a community an organization, its culture, and its people.

The basic differences between types of interviews are the amount of structure and the number of people involved. "Focus groups" are essentially group interviews, for example. The dynamics and methods are different but the goals are identical.

Structured interviews In structured interviews, which tend to be the most common in organizational work, the interviewer has a list of questions to make sure certain topics are covered. The person being interviewed, however, can cover whatever ground they like. (Usually, there are questions specifically designed to let the person choose their own topics). The advantage of structured interviews is that they allow the exploration of specific topics, while allowing people to tell the interviewer what they think is important. Common questions ask what is going well and what is going poorly; what motivates people; how they like their job, their peers, and their supervisor; the goals of their organization; the obstacles to performance and success; and what it takes to get ahead. One question we usually ask is what people would to if they had complete power to change any and all parts of the organization -- the "kind for a day" question.

Most questions have "probes" -- follow-up questions that bring out more information. Even when there are no formal probes, the interviewer usually asks people to elaborate further, and should make sure the person is completely done with one topic before moving to another. Some people need more prompting than others.

While when an interview can be handled by phone, more information is usually given in person.

Unstructured interviews

Sometimes, the interviewer wants to let a person have complete control over the content of the interview. One or two questions may be used to start off, but from then on, the only questions are probes, where the interviewer asks for more elaboration.

Fixed-response interviews

These are basically surveys without pencil or paper. They were used extensively in social science research during the 1950s and 1960s, and may help in exploring sensitive subjects where response rates are low or where people tend to respond different in person versus on paper.

Social welfare administration

Every profession needs some skills and techniques to achieve certain goals. In the field of social welfare, we need effective services, e.g. the diagnostic, prevention and curative or rehabilitation.

For the readjustment of destitute person and all handicapped persons, various social welfare agencies render services for this purpose.

Task of Administration:

The task of administration is to implement the agency programme effectively and sincerely. Social welfare administration can be called a process of transforming social policies and objective into social action.

Administration is a group progress:

Basically the administration is essentially a group process and revolves round the people who are implementing the programme at different levels which means that this is the process of working with groups of people. The knowledge and skills of the people working in the agency, their qualities and capabilities, and their approach and attitude will determine the quality of the programme they are able to put through. The success of the agency programme is clear indication of the success of agency administration.

Major aspects of Administration:

1. **Organizations and structure:** It includes the head of administration and other staff members.

2. **Policy making and planning:** It includes the various procedures and programmes for getting the goals in a better way.

3. **Programme Development:** It includes the use of various methods and techniques to achieve these goals.

4. **Function of the Executive boards:** It shows the responsibilities of the individuals and every member in given some responsibilities and functions for which he is responsible.

5. **Coordination:** It is needed for the smooth functioning of an organization and for the checking of duplication and overlapping etc.

6. **Supervision:** It is the duty of the good administrative to supervise all the activities going on under his administration, for this purpose he can nominate certain comities also.

7. **Proper Budgeting:** The good administrator has the quality of maintenance of the resources and the good budgeting. They have to look into available resources and expected expenditure of the programme and prepare the budget.

8. **Maintenance of Proper record:** In good administration, proper record keeping is given very much importance because it is very much needed for the smooth running of the programme. We know the present situation as well as the past situation and the plan for the future.

Importance:

1. social welfare administration is a process of transforming social policies and objective in to social action. For this purpose effective services are needed to achieve the goal.

2. In the field of social welfare administration these ends include rendering of effective services in the shape of diagnostic, curative or rehabilitative and preventive measures, for the uplifts of the maladjustment, physically handicapped and destitute persons of the society.

3. Every social welfare agencies have their own objectives and services. Presently in Pakistan, there are about twenty thousand such types of NGOs providing services to the needy persons.

4. The importance of social welfare administration has increased in welfare organizations. The following are some of the points which further show the importance of social welfare administration:

5. As social welfare has taken the form of organization actively for the solution of various social problems and in this connection the types of services provided by them are so complex that these agencies need coordination with other agencies also.

6. The success of programmes can only be ensured through good administration of social welfare agencies, which run on some sound and scientific lines.

7. As these programmes are very much complete in their nature so they need qualified and trained social workers to manage the affairs of agencies.

8. Social welfare administration having some knowledge regarding the principle of social worker's sympathetic attitude towards the people and their experience in dealing with the person's problems. For this purpose social worker is found a best administrator to achieve his goals.

9. Through social welfare administration, we easily gather the facts which identify the problems.

10. Through good administration, we can ensure the proper utilization of funds by a social welfare agency because the funds are utilized through effective methods with proper maintenance of accounts.

11. The good administration always evaluates its programme for judging the effectiveness of the programmes. Keeping in view, the changing needs of the society through evaluation of the programme. We can see the effecting of the techniques and skill applied in welfare programme and tries to further improve it.

Social action

The term social action refers to organized and legally permitted activities designed to mobilize public opinion, legislation and public administration in favor of objectives believed to be socially desirable.

Methods of Social Action:

☐ The following are some of the means, which make social action possible.

☐ Research and collection of data

☐ Planning solution, and arousing public opinion

☐ Meeting key persons, groups and agencies

☐ Public meetings

☐ Social education

☐ Propaganda

☐ Discussion

☐ Enlisting public support

☐ Coordinating the work of different groups and agencies

☐ Presentation of the proposal to those in authority

☐ Use of press if possible and meeting members of legislature

☐ Social legislation

☐ Enforcement of legislation

☐ Case work

Process of social action (Steps in social research)

First stage is of developing awareness among people of the problems and conditions, which limit social function as also of their causes. The tactics employed at this stage are of research and education. A social actionist, in order to find out facts relating to social reality so that sound conclusions may be arrived at, undertakes scientific social survey and research. After the knowledge of basic social issues confronting the life of people become available, it is disseminated to people in order to make them aware of these issues and problems. It is this stage that social actionists make use of various media, methods and techniques of communication to create awareness in the most effective manner. **Development of suitable organization** with clear-cut roles and responsibilities is the second stage in the process of social action. It is at this stage that efforts are made by the social actionist to mobiles as also to develop leadership enjoying the trust and confidence of the people. Cooperation and representation are the main techniques employed by the social actionist at this stage that tries to establish contacts with different sections make his best efforts to enlist their cooperation and involves them in the organization, which is created for effecting the desired changes. **After the establishment of necessary organization** comes the stage of formulation and projecting the goals and the strategies that are to be used for their effective attainment. In order to formulate goals, which should reflect the felt, needs of people, free and frank discussion with representatives of different sections in the organization is arranged and finally making suitable adjustments arrives at consensus. **The last stage in the social process** is of actual action in which the joint action incorporating fullest possible cooperation of all concerned is mobilized in order to attain the stipulated goals.

UNIT- IV FIELD OF SOCIAL WORK:

Social work practice widely used in almost all fields starting from industries, hospitals, corruptional settings, social settings etc,

Social work is a profession for those with a strong desire to help improve people's lives. Social workers help people function the best way they can in their environment, deal with their relationships, and solve personal and professional problems. Social workers practice in a variety of settings. Hospitals and psychiatric facilities they provide or arrange for a range of support services. In mental health, community centers, and private practice they provide counseling services on marriage, family, and adoption matters, and they help people through personal or community emergencies, such as dealing with loss or grief or arranging for disaster assistance. Industrial social work is one of the area in which the social worker extend their skill and expertness in helping personnel managers in the industry directly and organizational development indirectly, by intervening the employee management.

SOCIAL WORK IN INDUSTRIAL SETTING:

Industrial organization forms a secondary setting for the proactive of professional social work. It is different from other secondary welfare setting due to its primary orientation to production and profit rather than to the welfare needs of the workers. There is a growing recognition of the fact that the human personality is influenced by and influences the organization. Hence it is necessary to have a basic understanding of organizational structure of the industry in relation to its communication pattern and its system of authority. The workers and the problems can be better perceived against the holistic background of his work place, his work family, and his community. The industrial social worker whose work covers an intangible output can work with conviction and commitment in a profit oriented setting only if his/her functions are balanced with the primary interest of the organization. A clear understanding of the social workers role responsibilities and status in relation to the concerned department of great relevance. Although it was felt earlier that a personnel or welfare programmes need not have any connection with the economic potentials of the industry. It is increasingly felt that "A well formulate Social Work Practice," is as much as economic proposition as production or sales programme. It helps to improve the attitude of employees towards their job. As in the ultimate analysis it is the attitude of employees, which control the quality of production, quantity of the production and the productivity. Improvement in the attitude improves productivity and there by increases profit.

Role of Industrial Social Worker

It is essential to understand the areas of responsibilities associated with each functionary, so as to gain a clear perspective of role and status of the industrial social worker. The development of the industrial social work in India is recent. It is primarily voluntary and is influenced by the emphasis placed by the government on certain programmes in organized sector.

The place of social worker in an industrial organization is within the administrative preview of Personnel or Human Resource Management department. Occasionally is under the direct control of the line managers. The workers are occasionally involved in the decision making in the development of the welfare services. However, since he/she is enjoys autonomy in their day-to-day functioning, they are in a position to build a purposeful relationship with the operative employees. This will enable them to relate freely to the social worker with trust and confidence.

Professional Social Work Ethics

It is at this point that the issue of professional social work ethics assumes importance, both for the social worker and the employing organization.

1. The social worker should be outside the chain of command of the management, even though officially she may have to operate from the personnel or administrative department.

2. The worker should not have any responsibility involving his functionary, directly controlling the work life of the employee in so far as it affects the production process.

3. The worker should maintain the professional confidentiality. This does not mean that the worker should not share the workers problem with staff at other levels and management.

His work necessarily demands contact with different levels of management in the industry for effective discharge of his functions.

It is equally important for the workers to note that 'the strategic role of social worker in industry stem from his intimate contact with the rank and file workers as well as the access he has to in decision making channel and the upper echelons of the power structure in industry... but he should be very cautious of the dangers involved in his multiple identification with people in a variety of status of roles and in having his skills used manipulatively.

This is particularly true of his role in enhancing positive communication between workers and managers. This is highly complex, due to the growing importance of the trade unions, which now has great influence on the management. It is primarily delegated to the Personnel Officer and rather than to the Labor welfare Officer, or the social worker. It is the personnel officer who has to act as spokes men of the workers and advice the management on the action to be taken on their problem. He also have to strive to maintain a neutral stand to hold the balance between the management and employees and the situation which can arise possible conflicts between the trade unions and the management objectives. Here the positive and the neutral stand of the industrial social worker can be of great value to the personnel officer.

The responsibility of the social worker fall mainly in the category of non-statutory services such as:

1. Family individual and group, counselling and home visit in relation to adjustment of the work orientation, personality and other problems at preventive level.

2. Active participation in corporate social responsibility activities and community development initiatives of the industry.

3. Employee management and effective intervention of labour management problems.

4. Industrial counselling.

5. Case work interventions.

6. Health and educational help, which would involve referral to other agencies.

7. Coordination of welfare services with other welfare agencies.

8. Workers education.

9. Family planning and Family life education.

10. Workers recreation management.

Although personnel officer welfare officer and the industrial social worker are all concerned with the human relation aspect in the industry, a comparison of their rights and duties reveal that the former are organization oriented and the social worker is essentially employee oriented. He/she can effectively sustain her working relation with other specialist for implementing the social welfare policy.

Qualities of Industrial Social worker

The knowledge and personality traits deemed essential in a social worker in the industry are:

* Maturity

* Warm and genuine interest in people adjustability

* Good communication skills in dealing with people at different levels

* Resourcefulness

* Sound physical health

* Effective intervention skills

* Knowledge of industrial psychology

* Knowledge of labor laws

* Expertness in corporate-community interaction

* Expertness in industrial counselling

The industrial social worker with his basic knowledge of human dynamics and her skill in working with individuals at different levels will be a great asset in individualization service. The industrial social worker has to project his or her role as helper/moderator/facilitator rather than management appointed person. An ongoing coordination between training in social work institutions and industries is necessary and useful for effective feedback. Industrial social work should emerge as an accepted professional filed in India that will enable Human Resource Managers and Personnel Managers in the effective employee management and organizational development.

Social Work in Hospital settings

Social workers play a critical role in hospital settings by helping patients and families address the impact of illness and treatment. Tremendous stress often stems from hospitalizations that are sudden and, at times, related to catastrophic illness or injury. Stressors such as decreased personal control, information overload, change in functional ability and reduced financial resources, can lead to a range of emotional responses such as, anxiety, anger, and depression. Social workers, as part of the health care team, provide assessment and appropriate interventions to aid the patient in achieving optimum recovery/rehabilitation and quality of life. This includes maximizing the benefit the patient and family receive from their medical treatments and transitioning to risk-reduced, timely discharge. Social workers often have specific expertise in areas such as general medicine, emergency work, pediatrics, geriatrics, oncology, neurology, psychiatry, and palliative and end-of-life care.

The scope of practice of social workers entails "the assessment, diagnosis, treatment and evaluation of individual, interpersonal and societal problems to assist individuals, families, groups, communities and organizations to achieve optimum psychosocial and social functioning". The goal of social work practice is to restore, maintain and enhance social functioning by mobilizing strengths, supporting coping capacities, modifying dysfunctional patterns of relating and acting, linking people to necessary resources, alleviating environmental stressors and providing psychosocial education related to wellness and subjective well- being.

Core Social Work Skills Include the Ability to:

- ☐ Assess the bio psychosocial and ethno cultural needs of the patient, family and support system.
- ☐ Assess community and other large system factors impacting on patient health and treatment.
- ☐ Provide psychosocial interventions that facilitate patient and family adaptation and well-being.
- ☐ Facilitate family and team communication.
- ☐ Advocate for required services and navigate complex social systems.
- ☐ Provide crisis intervention and mediate conflict.
- ☐ Locate and negotiate potential resources.
- ☐ Educate patients and families on effective ways to mobilize existing resources.
- ☐ Develop and implement appropriate discharge plans/complete long-term care placement forms.

Social Workers Provide -

Social workers in health care commonly provide individual, couple, group and family counselling, crisis intervention, patient/family education, resource referral and advocacy, in inpatient and outpatient settings. Because social workers can provide both psychosocial care and other services to the patient and family, duplication of services is reduced. A mutually developed care plan for each patient/family is based on skillful psychosocial assessment. Consultation with medical and allied health professionals is implicit in developing and implementing treatment plans. Social work services can include all or some of the following: Psychosocial Assessment: screen for high-risk; determine need/eligibility for services; identify strengths/coping capacities; assess informal network of support. Counselling/Psychotherapy: assess role of emotional and social/cultural factors on health status and behavior and provide appropriate intervention; enhance coping capacities related to feelings of loss, grief and role changes; assess and intervene related to mental health concerns such as anxiety, depression, anger management.

Patient/Family Education: educate patients and families to facilitate understanding of hospital processes; increase understanding of illness/disability on relationships; and facilitate life transitions when health conditions require a modified lifestyle. Resource Counselling and Discharge Planning: identify and address barriers to discharge; locate resources; identify options and available supports; facilitate referrals and applications to government/community agencies; advocate for access to resources; coordinate referrals and/or placement plans; assist patient and family to emotionally prepare for transitions; prevent readmissions for non-medical reasons. Supportive Care to Outpatients: assist outpatients to identify and receive appropriate resources and supports, thus enabling increased compliance with treatment and preventing crisis or unnecessary hospital admission. Consultation: provide expertise/serve as a resource to interdisciplinary teams.

Social work in correctional settings

Social Work seeks to enhance the social functioning of individuals, singly and in groups, by activities focused upon their social relationships, which constitute the interaction between man and his environment. The activities can be grouped into three functions: restoration of impaired capacity, provision of individual and social resources and prevention of social dysfunction." Hence, social work is a discipline, which takes preventive and remedial action on problems in several areas of society. It helps families in economic or emotional difficulty. It works in medical, and school situations. It seeks to correct the causes underlying delinquency and crime. The three functions of social work, restoration of impaired capacity, provision of individual and social resources and prevention of social dysfunction, are intertwined and interdependent.

Restoration can be curative or rehabilitative. Its curative aspects are to eliminate factors, which have caused breakdown of functioning, and its rehabilitative aspects are toorganize and rebuild inter-factional patterns. Provision of resources can be developmental and educational. The developmental aspects are designed to further the effectiveness of existing social resources or to bring to full use the personal abilities for more effective social interaction. The educational aspect is structured to make familiar the public with specific conditions and needs for now or with changing social resources.

Prevention of social dysfunction involves early discovery, control, and elimination of conditions and situations, such as delinquency and crime, which potentially couldhamper effective social functioning. The two main divisions of prevention of social dysfunction are prevention of problems in the area of interaction between individuals and groups and secondly the prevention of social ills.

The underlying assumptions of social work in corrections settingsc) assumptive knowledge (or "Practice wisdom") that requires transformation into hypothetical and then into tested knowledge. The correctional social worker uses all three types of knowledge, and carries a professional responsibility for knowing, at any time, which type of knowledge he is using and what degree of scientific certainty is attached to it.

6) The knowledge needed for social work practice is determined by its goals and functions and the problems it seeks to solve and, hence, they are applicable in the administration of correction.

7) The internalization of professional knowledge and values is a vital characteristic of the professional social worker, since he is himself the instrument of professional help and he helps the offender to change his behavior.

8) Professional skill is expressed in the activities of the social worker. It constitutes his artistic creation, resulting from three internal processes: first, conscious selection of knowledge pertinent to the professional task at hand in order to help the offender, second, fusion of this knowledge with social work and correctional values; and third, the expression of this synthesis in professionally relevant activity to administer correction and to modify offending behavior. are:

1) Social Work, like all other professions, has problem solving functions and hence, it can help offenders in their treatment and rehabilitation.

2) Social Work practice is an art with a scientific and value foundation and, hence, correctional work is professional in nature.

3) Social Work as a profession came into being and continued to develop because it meets human needs and aspirations recognized by society. Hence, it assumes some of the socialization and control functions of society and helps the offenders to reshape their behavior.

4) Social Work practice takes its values from those held by the society of which it is a part. However, its values are not necessarily or altogether those universally or predominantly held or practiced in society and hence, it emphasizes in treatment and rehabilitation of the offender.

5) The scientific base of social work consists of three types of knowledge:

a) Tested knowledge,

b) Hypothetical knowledge that requires transformation into tested knowledge, andc) assumptive knowledge (or "Practice wisdom") that requires transformation into hypothetical and then into tested knowledge. The correctional social worker uses all three types of knowledge, and carries a professional responsibility for knowing, at any time, which type of knowledge he is using and what degree of scientific certainty is attached to it.

6) The knowledge needed for social work practice is determined by its goals and functions and the problems it seeks to solve and, hence, they are applicable in the administration of correction.

7) The internalization of professional knowledge and values is a vital characteristic of the professional social worker, since he is himself the instrument of professional help and he helps the offender to change his behavior.

8) Professional skill is expressed in the activities of the social worker. It constitutes his artistic creation, resulting from three internal processes: first, conscious selection of knowledge pertinent to the professional task at hand in order to help the offender, second, fusion of this knowledge with social work and correctional values; and third, the expression of this synthesis in professionally relevant activity to administer correction and to modify offending behavior.

These assumptions constitute commitments for the social worker. It also means that the functions assigned to social work by society represent a two-fold responsibility. The first is to determine the professional activities through which it seeks to reach its socially approved goals and modify them as necessary in the light of changing social needs. The second is to exercisediscipline and control over practice that would keep its professional accountability. A problem developed in the area of social interaction, whether raised as a problem by the individual or by a group in the community, calls for the professional services of the social worker.

In correction, Social Work not only helps individuals, groups and community to solve problems, but also assists them to prevent offending behavior and enrich daily living. So, the main focus of the social worker is upon helping people to prevent and control crime. The social worker usually works with clients on a conscious level, helping them to face realities and solve problems in preventing and controlling offending behaviors.

In correction, Social Work is an art because it requires great skills to understand delinquent and criminal behavior. It is a science because of its problem-solving method and its attempt to be objective in determining delinquent and criminal activities and in developing principles and operational concepts to deal with delinquency and crime. It is a profession because it encompasses the attributes of a profession in dealing with offending behavior.

Values of Social Work in Correction

Social work values are basically the values of democratic societies, which are mainly the worth of the individual, the inherent dignity of the human person, society's responsibility for contributing to the common good, etc. For the National Association of Social Workers, the following six values are listed basic to the practice of social work:

1) The individual is the primary concern of this society.

2) There is interdependence between individuals in this society.

3) They have social responsibility towards one another.

4) There are human needs common to each person, yet each person is essentially unique and different from others.

5) An essential attribute of a democratic society is the realization of the full potential of each individual and the assumption of his social responsibility through active participation in society.

6) Society has a responsibility to provide ways in which obstacles to this self-realization can be

overcome or prevented.

Correctional Settings and Task of Social Workers

To deal with officially identified delinquents and criminals, every democratic society has created a system of correctional agencies. These agencies have been given the task of administering the penalties assigned to delinquents and criminals. These agencies are expected to protect the community during the offender's period of supervised status by controlling his behavior. Furthermore, they are expected to help the offender, so that he can return to normal status, better able to be a constructive member of the community.

Probation and Parole are the two main agencies in the correctional system. Different kinds of correctional institutions are as follows:

- Prisons
- Borstal Schools
- Schools for Juvenile Delinquents
- Remand/Observation Homes
- Beggar Homes
- Reception Centers, Protective Homes
- State Homes, Probation Hostels

The nature of the penalties, which these agencies administer, is essentially that of a handicapped personal and social status. This period of down-graded status is spent under supervision either in an institution or in the community under the guidance of a correctional social worker.

Social work through NGOs

Social work and non-governmental organizations — also known as NGOs — are concepts which are often linked, and yet the two represent fundamentally different ideas. The key difference between social work and NGOs is that social work is a field of study and practice, whereas NGOs are a type of organization. NGOs can often carry out social work, but not all NGOs are involved in social work and a great deal of social work is done by organizations which are not NGOs.

"NGOs are bodies which are neither government agencies nor businesses. The term can refer to a wide variety of different types of organization, but it often describes charitable or advocacy groups such as Amnesty International or the International Red Cross. The term most commonly applies to international organizations, although this usage varies; there is no universal definition of an NGO. NGOs address a wide variety of issues, including economic and technological development, disaster relief, animal welfare and other global problems.

Like "NGO," "social work" is a term which covers a wide range of activities. Broadly speaking, social work refers to programs intended to improve the welfare and living conditions of members of society, particularly low-income or otherwise marginalized communities. Social work can involve education, counseling, political advocacy, career development and any other activity which aims to improve the life of an individual or community.

As we have seen, NGOs are often involved in charitable or advocacy work, both of which play a role in social work. In this respect, then, there is a clear link between social work and NGOs. Some NGOs are involved in activities that are closely related to social work.

The link between social work and NGOs, although close, is not consistent. Governments are one of the major providers of social work, with government-employed social workers attempting to address issues such as child abuse, poverty and other issues. Since many social workers are employed by the government, it is clear that not all social work is performed by NGOs.

Just as not all social work is performed by NGOs, not all NGOs perform social work. Although the relationship between social work and NGOs is close, some NGOs perform other functions.

For example, the World Wide Fund for Nature is a well-known and influential NGO which addresses environmental issues, particularly the question of endangered species. Since it is working for the well-being of the environment, and only indirectly for the welfare of human communities, this NGO is not involved in social work.

Unit – V RECENT TRENDS

Field work and its importance to social work education – transactional analysis for social work practice – the concept of integrated social work approach – the problems and prospects of the profession – the future of social work.

Importance of Field Work in Social Work Education

Field work is important that students should be helped to develop the attitude of mind ideas them to make connections between study & relief…it is needed vital that this should be done if students are to become professional practitioners in the field rather than goods nature & amateurs of techniques applying narrow skills by rule of thumbs method. (Robert, 1995)

Field practicum is a dynamic course that challenges students to apply social work knowledge, skills & values within an organizational context. It is a vital dimension of students graduate & post graduate social work education.

In "Field Work manual" M.A. Momin has mentioned the following importance of field work practice:

- Through the field work, the students can learn how to apply social work methods in the situation of given individuals, groups or communities problems.

- They are exposed to agency practice in which they are in systematically, preplanned approach to solve problem process such as study, diagnosis & treatment.

- The students achieve self-awareness & discipline to use them as a helper & as agent of change in an individual & group situation.

- The students develop facility in the use of organizational structure. They come to know foster & use relationship within a structure & gain insight regarding his/her network of relationship in the organization.

- It helps the students to apply the students to apply the theory & principle of social work into actual practice.

- The students acquire social work knowledge & are given an opportunity to try variety of social work methods, skills & technique.

- The students become familiar with administrative procedure & process. They learn how to run an office, what kind of routine needs to be established, how to facilitate administrative arrangement, relevant to the discharge of the responsibilities of their own assignment.

- The students have an opportunity to learn the organizational framework of services. They understand structure & policy & how to facilitate such policy through practice. They become familiar with difference institutional styles & tempos of agencies associated with various field practices.

- The students acquire significant substance substitute knowledge in the specified field of practice characterized by the agency. They become acquire with causes of the problem & with social welfare programs, agency structure, laws, & policies, related to its solution.

- The students acquire knowledge regarding community structure and process. They know the kinds of formal & group & force that a community. They should have to ability to utilize community resources in support of social welfare.

Inter-relationship between Social Work Education and Field Work

Modern social work education has two dimensions: theoretical and practical. A social worker gains knowledge about society, social problems, property, social structure, social values, human behavior, social work process when practical training enable them to use this knowledge acquired knowledge in this field for real life purposes. Thus practical training is required for social worker to solve social problems of human beings/society for modern social work.

Taking notice of this requirement higher education has been provided with practical training course in its syllabus about social work, through which students can apply theoretical knowledge for solution of problems. Social and Economic Council of United Nations has recognized social work as a profession in 1951 and formulated the following decisions. Social Work is a profession based on trained male and female and who are obtained theoretical and practical knowledge in social work degree from established and recognized educational institutions is mandatory to fulfill by them.

Social Work is a practical education, which is learned through theoretical study of society and social work. This is because 'public good' can be affected only by applying theoretical knowledge in real life in a scientific way. And practical training helps apprentices to be full-hedged social workers by making arrangements of applying theoretical knowledge in practical life. And these together make social work education and practical training inter-dependent upon each other.

CREATOR	T.M.SURESH
ABOUT PROJECT MSW	CONVERSION OF SOCIAL WORK STUDY MATERIALS (IN PAPER) INTO SOFT COPIES, ELIMINATING THE DIFFUCILTIES IN GETTING STUDY MATERIALS.
WANT TO JOIN PROJECT MSW	EMAIL US TO \htms3292@gmail.com0R CALL US AT 91-9626633799.

www.ingramcontent.com/pod-product-compliance
Lightning Source LLC
Chambersburg PA
CBHW071056290526
45795CB00004B/1523